Thomas Keith Tindale
South Hanover
November, 1967.

Highway to the Wilderness

Highway

WALTER BACON

o the Wilderness

Illustrated and with Maps

The Vanguard Press, Inc. / *New York*

CONTENTS

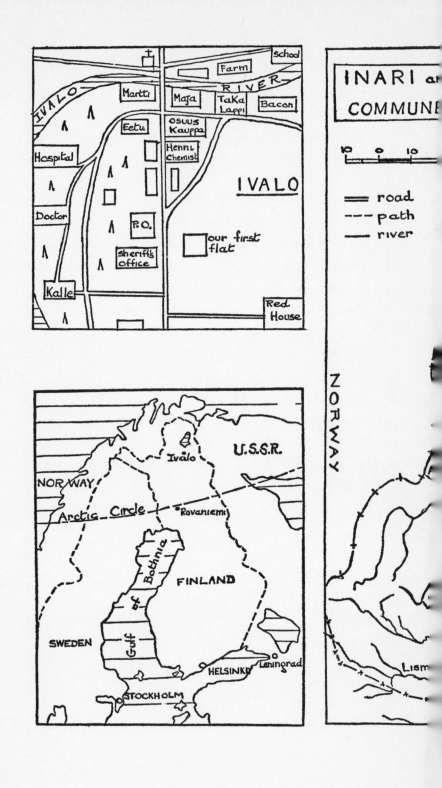

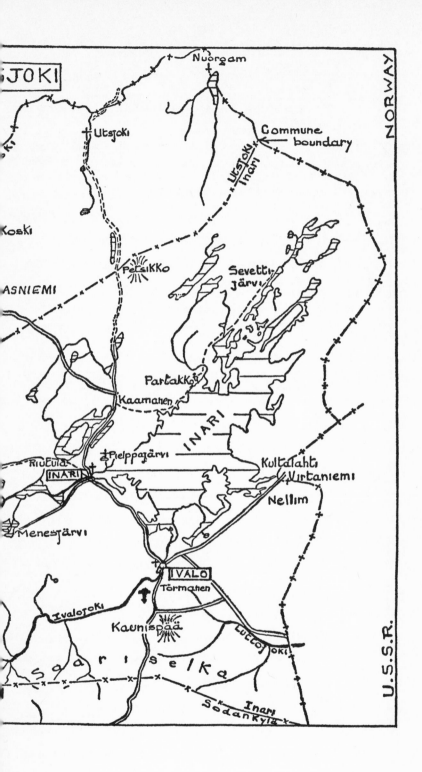

ACKNOWLEDGEMENTS

FIRST of all to Arja, for without her this book would not have been written at all. She not only provided a good deal of the material for me to write about but made many sacrifices so that this could be done, and finally worked unceasingly at the not very thankful task of criticizing what had been written.

Secondly the people of Lapland, especially our friends in Inari commune—it would be difficult to mention them individually—who took us so generously to their hearts and whom we shall not forget.

Finally I should like to thank Ilona Kaukoranta-Ilveskivi and Eetu Saarelainen for permission to reproduce photographs and Miss Mary Smithies and Miss Barbara Sullivan for their advice and assistance in the preparation of the manuscript. And if the book had a dedication, it would be: to the independent man—or woman.

Note: "Lapp" has been used throughout this book, since it is a commonly known word, but the real name for the Lapps —and the one by which they would prefer to be called—is "Saami".

ILLUSTRATIONS

1 : *Journey into Darkness*

WE WENT to Lapland in 1955 and did not leave it till the end of 1958, though originally we had not intended to stay longer than a few months. On the surface, our going there seemed to be by chance, a hasty reaction to a sudden impulse; but the forces which took us had been developing in our lives for years.

After we had come back, after we had left behind the reindeer and the northern lights, the long nights of winter and the overwhelming sunshine of summer, I started to write. I planned a factual and detached account of Lapland and its inhabitants. But, as I wrote, I realized that to do so was to leave the heart out. It was to leave out the strange compelling force which exists in Lapland. For while, in the imagination of some, Lapland is a place of darkness and cold, of loneliness and hardship and to go there would be to go into exile, to others it is like a magnet. Why are they attracted by it? "Because the air is purer and the waters are clearer and the sky is bluer than anywhere else," said an old Lapp woman, when asked why she insisted on returning to the hard Arctic life instead of remaining in the comfort of the south to which she had been taken. She went back, and others of her race did the same; though some had seen their homes twice destroyed they returned to build them for the third time.

The old Lapp woman was going to her homeland; but others, to whom it was not home, have also been drawn there—and sometimes drawn back after they have tried to leave. To a man who likes shooting and fishing, Lapland has obvious attractions. But why should a pretty woman from a modern city choose to live, virtually cut off for several months of the year, in a remote Lappish village? And when she has turned her back on it and gone away, back to the south, what is it that drives her to return?

Lapland, the loneliest area in Europe, is a country of individuals; and a country where the individual is respected. Men think their own thoughts; but they allow to others the right to think differently. It is the interaction between these unique men and women and their lonely half wild environment which gives the life of Lapland its peculiar tang. The natural phenomena, the severe climate with its dramatic swing from sunless winter to unbounded summer light and the primitive

11

landscape, as untouched in places as though man had never been—these are half the picture. The other half is formed by the people themselves. What are the feelings which make them want to go and stay in this environment?

The pattern of events which was to take me to Lapland began to develop in 1952. There were, on the surface, no signs that any such venture was ever likely to take place. I had a secure niche as a lecturer in electronic engineering at a College of Technology on the south coast of England; and the major part of my life up to that time had been spent in laboratories and factories and classrooms, in steady unadventurous work in this field. I enjoyed teaching, particularly the more theoretical parts of the subject in which one moved steadily from one step to another until the whole underlying logic was revealed. I was also spending several hours a week on research.

I had not, however, settled down in the job at all: and yet I would have found it difficult to make clear all the stirrings which were going on in my mind. There was an element of personal ambition in it: a desire to create freely without the checks and trammels of a bureaucratic system, to lead rather than be led, and a longing for independence. But there was more than this, for independence might quite possibly have been achieved; but as I made various attempts to do so, I became conscious that there was a fatal division in me. I could not believe the result was worth the sacrifice necessary to attain it—not, that is, so long as I stayed solely in electronics. In our technical civilization I was, I realized, a heretic and a deviationist.

Engineering exists "for the comfort and convenience of mankind". These are both desirable objects, but hardly sufficient as the end of all existence. Yet if one analyzes the promises made by the politicians and the offers of advertisers, there seems to be little more than this which they have in mind. To increase the "comfort and convenience" of that half of mankind which is in want—that would be worth doing; but to devote the whole of one's energy to adding gadgets and refinements to our already highly developed way of life is like taking coals to Newcastle. There are other things which are more necessary. So I thought.

With this went another, more disturbing, reaction; a reaction, apparently, against the whole environment in which I had been brought up, the very environment which supported my profession—a reaction against the city. I had always lived, or worked, in a city of at least a quarter of a million people. But now the hard stone and steel streets, the great buildings with their long rigid corridors, seemed like a trap—a press that

stamped men into its own mould and destroyed their indivi-
duality. It seemed, now that I had recognized it, that this
reaction had been with me a very long time, though only at last
seen clearly. I wondered, at times, if any faint inheritance from
one's ancestors could produce such feelings: my grandfather
was a cottager in a tiny village in Lincolnshire. At other times,
I suspected that this was more than any personal longing: that
cities, as we know them, do some real violence to man's true
nature.

I became increasingly suspicious of the specialized studies I
was making. They were, without doubt, fascinating. Electronics is developing with explosive rapidity: each month,
each week almost, there was some new circuit or idea which
ought to be analyzed. One couldn't, however, leave it there.
The analysis suggested further questions. Could we do it this
way and get a revolutionary improvement? Could we work out
the theory further? And over lunch or on the train and sometimes into the night one's mind went on working. It was ex-
hilarating, a special private world which you could take with
you and retire into when the ordinary world was difficult or
boring. A good many times I liked it, but sometimes I would
wake up and see myself as a man growing steadily older, who
sat in a basement room with a green table between giving lec-
tures—a room growing steadily smaller and smaller until
finally there was nothing left in it, no music, no beauty, no real
but painful world at all, nothing but electronic circuits. At
such times, the sign on the back entrance through which I normally came in, an entrance which the College shared with
another city institution, seemed to have a sinister appropriate-
ness: TURN LEFT FOR THE MORTUARY.

There remained the vacations, and I resolved to use these as
far as possible creatively. I had for some years been sympathetic
to the outlook of the Society of Friends, or Quakers, and in the
summer of 1952 I went to a seminar in Holland organized by
the American Friends' Service Committee; and that affected
the whole course of my life. One day I explained the background of thinking which had brought me to the seminar to a
small, fair-haired Finnish girl called Arja Aromaa. She said:
"I have some of the same feelings. I have a profession—quite a
good profession—but it doesn't satisfy me. I've been to several
A.F.S.C. work camps, including one in America. I've helped to
lead some."

We spent a good deal of time together during the seminar,
and towards the end she impulsively said to me: "Why not
come to Helsinki for Christmas?"

Sometimes, when one comes for the first time to a new place there is a sudden sharp reaction of like or dislike. One tries to keep it down, to wait until one has had time for a mature judgment, yet the feeling persists: and occasionally it is right, a genuine instinctive knowledge of what is going to be significant in the future. I reached Helsinki by plane. We flew steadily over the innumerable islands that stretch across the Gulf of Bothnia as though scattered by some giant salt cellar, snow-covered land alternating with frozen sea, until finally the tiny houses below began to appear in clusters and strings instead of standing as isolated specks in the whiteness. The plane dropped down and landed. I walked out on to the hard frosty landing field, looked across it to the forest round its rim, and thought: This place is for me.

Like most people who visit Helsinki for the first time in winter, I had brought layers of woollen underwear; and I perspired freely as we jammed ourselves into the crowded trams, their doors closed so firmly against the outer atmosphere, or went from one centrally heated building to the next. The traffic roared down the broad streets past the tall blocks of flats, and the synthetic Christmas music floated over the strings of lights in Aleksanterinkatu—the Regent Street of Helsinki. One would have to go further than Helsinki to escape civilization, and I realized that Arja was almost as much a product of it as I was.

Yet sometimes at night when the others had gone to bed I would stand at the window staring alternately at the lines of cars left out in the freezing night, and at a picture on the wall. It was a picture of a farm, a Finnish farm with the wooden farm buildings, the cleared fields, and all round it—pushed back a little—the forest. It seemed to me then that somewhere in this Finland men and women might be closer to something we had forgotten, strong, primitive, perhaps fierce.

We were married in the summer of 1954 and settled down in a small picturesque house in Haslemere. We planned to stay in England. In the spring of 1955, Arja went to see the doctor. "All right, you can start knitting," he said laconically. We decided that Arja should go to Helsinki to have the baby, which was due in September. There are excellent hospitals in Finland in which the cost of treatment is not high; and, apart from that, it is more comfortable to be dealt with at such a time by people who speak one's own language.

Unknown to us, however, this decision had altered the whole direction in which we were going. Arja left in May; I followed in July, and we spent the summer at Viittakivi, a Folk High

School on the edge of Lake Kirrinen in the pleasant Häme country about ninety miles from Helsinki. I lectured there during July and August to summer course students learning English. As the water in the lake began to grow cold for swimming and the first nip of autumn was in the air, we returned to Helsinki. "How about going to live in Ivalo?" asked Arja one day, looking up from the Finnish paper *Uusi Suomi*.

"Where's Ivalo?"

"In Lapland."

I thought she was joking, and laughed.

"I'm serious." She handed the paper to me. "Inari commune are advertising for a school dentist."

Arja was a dentist; in Finland the majority of dentists are women. She had practised for a year or two before our marriage, but not whilst we had been living in England.

"You could teach English," she went on. "That would give you an income. There are bound to be a few people who want to learn, even there."

"Who, for example?"

"Oh, the teachers at the school, the doctor and the pastor perhaps—and others. You would have time for writing, too. Perhaps you could get material for a book on Lapland. We could go for a year and then come back, but we should have seen what Lapland really was like all the year round."

"You couldn't possibly manage it with a young child."

This was an unwise thing to say; to suggest to a Finn that some task is beyond him or her usually makes the hearer even more determined to do it.

"Of course I could," Arja replied a trifle angrily. "Most Finnish women do. I should get two girls to help and a young baby doesn't need much attention. It sleeps most of the time. I should have my surgery in the same building so it would be very easy to keep an eye on the baby."

This was good theory, and I had not then the experience to know how much this particular theory differed from practice.

"But isn't it very risky taking such a small child up there in that cold?"

"The Lapps have babies, don't they? Anyway, it would be inside most of the time. It would be as warm as though it were in England. It says here that a modern flat has been reserved for the dentist."

"Really?" I found it difficult to imagine what a modern flat in the middle of Lapland could be like.

"Yes. So we should be quite comfortable. Are you entirely against it? Shall I throw the advertisement away?"

"No," I said slowly. "Let's think it over." Actually, I was thrilled with the idea, but wanted to study the possible difficulties.

I looked for Ivalo on the map. A dotted line runs across the map of the world at 66° 32′ north—the Arctic Circle, north of which for some time each year the sun disappears completely below the horizon. Lapland is, broadly speaking, that part of Europe north of the Arctic Circle. It stretches across parts of Norway, Sweden, Finland, and the U.S.S.R. Finnish Lapland reaches up between Sweden and the U.S.S.R. with the end of Norway running round the top of it. We had spent a few days travelling down the western arm of Lapland before our marriage; not long, but enough to feel its strange attraction. The eastern side, however, I had not seen at all, and this was where Ivalo was situated.

The only towns of any size associated with Finnish Lapland are Kemi, Rovaniemi, and Kemijärvi; and the first two of these are south of the Arctic Circle. Kemi, with a population of 25,000, is the largest. The railway runs up the western side of Finland to Kemi; then one branch curves north round the end of the Gulf of Bothnia into Sweden, whilst the other branch turns right and goes through Rovaniemi and Kemijärvi to the Russian border.

North of these towns, the density of population falls to an average beneath two per square mile; and north of them, also, the railway ceases. The only way on is by road or by plane. But roads in Lapland are few. The main road from the south runs up along the valley of the Muonio River into Norway, with two connections to Rovaniemi. From Rovaniemi itself—referred to as the capital of Lapland—one road follows the railway line to the east, whilst the other runs north. About 200 miles north of the Arctic Circle there is a broad splash of blue on the map— Lake Inari (or Enare); shortly before this lake the road divides, one branch running to Russia and the Arctic Ocean, along the eastern side of the lake, whilst the other branch curves to the west and goes into Norway.

Where the road divided, there was a small dot on the map marked IVALO. The region round looked very empty; the road seemed like a highway to the wilderness. There was no place even as big as Ivalo to the north, whilst south, the next town was Sodankylä, about a hundred miles away. East and west, there appeared nothing but hills and rivers till the border was reached. It was difficult to see where even one person per square mile could live.

Small matters sometimes take an unexpectedly long time to

settle, whilst big ones are unexpectedly clear. We knew, in a few days, that we intended to go to Ivalo. The decision had been made, and what was left was the organization necessary to get us there.

That, however, was not so simple. Before leaving my work at the college, I had to give three months' notice and settle our affairs in England; whilst Arja, in addition to having the baby, had to create a dental surgery in Ivalo. The baby, which was due at the beginning of September, was late; and after waiting till the last possible day I set off back to England. The first result of our Lapland project was separation. It was a separation which made our early life in Lapland more difficult, since neither of us properly understood the experiences which the other had had during that time, and we approached Lapland with different points of view.

On the way back a telegram reached me: "JOAN LILIAN BORN TODAY; 3.7 kg., 51 cm." Up to that time, although I had wanted a child very much, I had been half afraid of the limitations it would impose; now that I had to think of a separate person with a name—Lilian—my feelings altered and the fears disappeared. I wanted to see her. I knew roughly when that would be, but I could not picture what the place would be like.

England was waiting, as it always had been waiting after the summer vacation. Students were queuing up outside the college, waiting to enroll; and on the staff we were working out timetables with the illusion, held every year, that this time it was going to be better organized, more smooth running, more like the ideal than it had ever been before. It seemed very solid, this life I had known for several years, the life I had lived before I was married, solid and dangerously real: dangerous because its commonplaceness made the Lapland adventure like a dream. It was difficult to believe that before Christmas this life would dissolve, that I should be living in a strange country in totally different circumstances; difficult to believe that I had a wife, and daughter I had never seen, in that distant Arctic town. If it had not been for the letters it would have been easy to suppose that the whole idea existed only in my imagination. But they came: "Today I went with Lilian by plane to Ivalo. It was the last plane of the summer. . . ." ". . . I have managed to get a girl to help, a shy Lappish girl called Fetsi. She makes simple but good food. . . ." ". . . the temperature here is minus twenty.* It is cold but very dry and beautiful. Yesterday I went to Kaunispää and did some ski-ing. How soon can you be here?"

It came as a slight shock to realize that I must decide what to

* Centigrade.

take, that I could not take very much, and that I should be, to a large extent, dependent on what I did take. Which books were so important that I must have them with me? Another problem was also absorbing every moment I could spare. I proposed to take my notebooks along with me to Lapland and write up the work I had been doing. I hoped to submit it for a higher degree of London University. The purely theoretical side of this could be finished anywhere; but it was absolutely essential that the experiments designed to try out this theory in practice should be finished. There was no possibility of electronics research in Lapland. I obtained the basic results I needed, though there was time for little more than the absolutely necessary minimum, and left the college with real regret at parting from many good friends.

I had arranged to sell the small house in Haslemere and put most of our belongings into stores. It was a decision that had a profound effect on my feelings in Lapland. I had burned my boats; there was no automatic way back. I filled three large boxes with odds and ends of my own, my wife's clothes, and her small dental instruments. I had had no experience of packing dental instruments for Lapland, and as far as I know there is no work in existence on the subject. However, the boxes later arrived safely with nothing broken except the glass in one picture.

To anyone faced with a similar problem I should recommend taking all the books you are likely to need, since these will not otherwise be readily available, a portable typewriter, and very little else. Clothing and other equipment is much better bought on the spot where they know the requirements.

I finished packing at 5 a.m. When day has succeeded day for so long with little change in the routine of life it is difficult to realize that one has come to a morning after which nothing will be the same. By the next evening the house was an empty shell. The following day the new owner moved in and as a parting gesture of goodwill gave me a lift to the station. The train roared in and stopped in the exact position in which long experience had taught me that it would stop. I pushed my suitcase into a crowded carriage and gave a last look at the woods and hills of Haslemere as they disappeared behind and the train carried me with increasing speed towards the plane for Copenhagen, Helsinki, and Rovaniemi.

2 : *Home in an Unknown Land*

THE girl behind the refreshment counter in the little airport glanced at the traveller. He didn't seem likely to order anything else. The plane, after its fifteen-minute stop, had hurried off back to Helsinki, the bus for Rovaniemi town had gone. The girl shut up the refreshment counter and disappeared into the room at the back. The traveller—myself—was left alone staring out of the window.

It seemed suddenly very quiet. A long piece of glass formed the whole of one wall; it showed an empty landing strip and a line of trees. Beyond that the hills of Lapland stretched out, mysterious, grey, and empty. On the other wall was a picture of a plane surrounded by reindeer; I wondered if it ever happened like that in reality.

It was two o'clock on a Saturday afternoon in the beginning of December. It had been almost foolishly easy to get here; two telephone calls and a cheque had fixed the plane tickets, and after that I had lived in the artificial world of air travel, passed along with great care from one airport to another almost exactly like it, as though I were a precious parcel. It had been so easy that I had forgotten, almost, that I was going away from the very society which had created the planes.

Now, in the profound silence, I felt as though I were suspended between the two worlds: behind, the world of cities and technical progress for which I had been conditioned, and ahead—the Arctic. I hoped I was going to like it.

The stillness was broken by the sound of a heavy motor vehicle outside. I walked quickly to the door. An orange bus with the sign of the posthorn was standing there. At that time the bus was the only means of public transport in winter between Rovaniemi and Ivalo, 180 miles away. The bus looked ominously full. The conductor climbed out and looked at me thoughtfully. "You will have to stay," he told me sadly.

My heart sank. When was the next bus? Was there another bus that day? How if that were full? How many days and nights might I stay at this airport before I found a bus prepared to take me north? But the conductor pushed me towards the door. "You will have to stay," he repeated, "there are no seats." After a second it occurred to me that he probably knew German as well as English, both of which languages are frequently spoken in Finland; English "stay" sounds like German "*stehen*" and is often used to mean "stand". So I pressed forward and wedged myself in between a woman with a large shopping basket and a row of boys sucking sweets. I was glad to be in the lifeboat, though I didn't fancy eight hours standing in a position which made me feel like a corkscrew. The bus was crammed with similar women with bursting baskets, with children swirling round them. Somehow I seemed to have escaped the Arctic and landed in the middle of a jolly Saturday afternoon shopping expedition.

Screwing my neck round I managed to see out of the window. There was still some light in the sky, but it would soon be gone. The snow had been pushed off the road into two long ridges, one on either side; past the ridges it stretched white and untouched between dark trees, green and brown. Occasionally the trees parted and the broad blank expanse of a frozen lake stood out.

The bus stopped at the end of a brown lane. A woman got out. She couldn't manage her parcels so the conductor helped her. She said something to him and they both laughed. I watched her disappear up the brown lane; there was a wooden house at the top, almost hidden in the trees. The bus went on again until it came to another brown lane. This time it didn't stop; instead it slowed down, the conductor leaned out and threw a parcel into a yellow box on top of a stick beside the road and the bus went on once more.

The distance between the stops got longer and longer. Many of the passengers had left and there were some seats free. I sat down beside a man with a dark coat and a fur hat. My feet were cold. The bus was warm, but some cold air came sneaking in along the floor every time the door was opened. I was wearing some lined boots which felt wonderful in London, but didn't seem able to keep out that Lapland draught. The man next to me kept looking at them. "You haven't got the right boots," he said at last, in Finnish. Luckily I knew a little. "Sit here. It's warmer." He changed places with me so that I could be next to the heater.

It was cosy next to the heater. I felt drowsy. Most of the other passengers seemed to be falling asleep also. The bus stopped again. It didn't start. I opened my eyes. A man was walking down between the seats. He didn't seem to like letting go of them and he couldn't always find where they were. He looked drunk. The bus still didn't start, and the man found a seat.

The driver came and took something from his hand. It was a bottle, about a quarter full of brownish liquid. The driver threw it out of the door and started the bus. The man didn't protest and in a little while was asleep. It was now completely dark and there was nothing to see so I drifted off to sleep also.

I was awakened abruptly. The bus was pulling into a lighted area. I could see houses and shops. "Don't worry if it's cold when you reach Sodankylä," my wife had written. "They say it's one of the coldest places in Lapland. It will be better when you get to Ivalo." I guessed this was Sodankylä. The bus had stopped outside a restaurant called the Café Polaris. It seemed an appropriate name.

I went in and ordered a ham omelette because I knew the word for it. A Norwegian girl was sitting at the same table. She'd heard a story that the bus wasn't going to go on any further. I didn't believe a Finnish bus would stop like that, but it worried me all the same, because at that moment the Café Polaris and the few lights round the square were the only things that were real. When you got past that there was the darkness, and to believe that there was anything beyond the darkness you had to use your imagination very hard and then you couldn't be sure that anything out there existed except in your imagination. There seemed no reason why anyone should want to leave the light and warmth and go out into the darkness and cold.

After a little while, however, the bus reappeared again and we climbed into it and went off. All we could see now was a patch of light moving along where the headlights from the bus struck the road. We went along for a long time and didn't stop. All at once the driver slowed the bus and called out to the conductor, "*Poroja!*" There were two reindeer on the road, looking as though they owned it. They moved off slowly as we came near to them. Shortly after this we saw a building, then another building, and then the bus stopped.

"Ivalo Post Office," said the conductor, looking at me. He got down and helped me take out my luggage from the back. We were standing between two buildings, both set well back from the road. Someone was coming out from the smaller building. It was Arja, my wife. I raised my black Homburg hat and stepped forward on to the pavement to meet her. There are no pavements at the side of the road in Lapland and I found myself plunging about undignifiedly in three feet of snow in a ditch.

I struggled out and followed Arja round to the back of the

house. A door led to the upper floor: stuck on it was a notice which said:

DENTIST AROMAA-BACON
APPOINTMENTS ONLY

We opened the door and went upstairs and into the flat in a glorious blaze of light. I felt as though I had been swimming on a great dark sea and at last had come to rest on a friendly island. The pictures in my mind were not mirages: this home in Lapland did exist. Arja led me gently into the bedroom. "There she is," she whispered.

I stared at the cot against the wall. A small golden-haired figure was sleeping in it. I had no idea that a three-months-old child could be so beautiful. She was so perfect and so still that she might have been a doll modelled by some superb artist. Then she moved slightly in her sleep. She was alive. She was real. This was Lilian.

Arja drew me quietly back into the main room of the flat.

"How do you like it?" she asked.

"The flat? I think it's wonderful. There's shaded electric lights and carpets and central heating and a flush toilet. It's luxury."

It was, indeed, very comfortable; not at all full of the primitive inconvenience which we had both expected when we first talked of coming to Lapland. The flat had not, however, been made like this without a struggle. Arja told me later the story of her arrival. She left Helsinki when Lilian was three weeks old. Planes flew from Helsinki to Rovaniemi throughout the year, but they only came as far as Ivalo during the summer. Arja and Lilian crossed the Arctic Circle on the very last plane of the summer; they had to come then or face eight or nine hours in the bus from Rovaniemi.

When she arrived and looked in the flat, Arja said, her heart sank. There was nothing except bare boards. For the first few days she went to stay in the flat of Eetu Saarelainen and his wife Maija. Eetu was the *kunnanjohtaja*, the chief executive officer of the local council, and it was he who was responsible for the appointment of Arja as school dentist. The commune lent her some furniture to begin with; the rest had to be ordered up and trickled in over a long period. As soon as there were beds, chairs, and a cooker in the flat Arja moved in. A square room at one corner of the flat near the steps had been set aside for a dental surgery.

Many country communes in Finland do not provide dental instruments, and the dentist has to bring her own. But Ivalo was generous. The commune bought a set of new equipment for the surgery and allowed Arja to choose everything she wanted without argument.

The dental chair and drill and other heavy pieces of equipment had to be carried upstairs and installed in the surgery, but when they arrived Arja hadn't even a tool to open the boxes, much less the strength to pick up several hundredweight of dental gear. It needed several men. In despair she went to the caretaker who lived on the ground floor. "That's all right," he said. "I'll get some of the boys round." Shortly afterwards a tough-looking crowd turned up, a selection of the wanderers who take casual jobs in Lapland and who didn't happen to have anything on at that moment. They lugged the dental machinery up the stairs and installed it in the surgery. Payment? No, that was quite all right, they didn't want anything.

Another combination of a sudden problem and ready help occurred a few nights later. Arja had gone to bed when she heard something hit the window. She listened, and a voice called: "Is that the dentist?" and then more urgently, "Is that *the dentist?*" Arja put her head out of the window. "I'm from Hammasväline," went on the voice. Hammasväline is a Finnish dental firm which had supplied the equipment. "I've come to set up your dental unit." (This is a specialized job which needs to be done by an expert.) "I've got to go first thing in the morning and I shall need some men to help me all night."

Arja put on a dressing gown and went to look for the caretaker. He was ready to go to bed and she approached him somewhat hesitantly. "You need someone to help?" he said. "I'll get the man from the telephone exchange." He came back a few minutes later with the other man and they worked throughout the night on the assembly of the dental chair. In the morning the man from the telephone exchange disappeared off to his own work. No, he said, he didn't want to take anything for helping the dentist to get established.

Arja stopped talking and I stared at the wood fire burning in a brick fireplace in one corner of the room. The fireplace wasn't necessary—the room was well warmed by central heating; but it was a very pleasant luxury to stare at and dream over, whilst I tried to visualize the pattern of life here and the struggle to build it up.

"There's some tea ready," Arja said to me. "But before that you must come into the kitchen. You have someone else to meet."

"Who is that?"

"Fetsi—the Lappish girl I told you about who is helping me."

We went into the kitchen, through a door which opened out of the bedroom. There was a white electric cooker with a water heater above it and a table on the opposite side with some cups on it. I'd seen many kitchens like it before. But I had never seen anybody quite like Fetsi. She was standing by the cooker when I went in; she was plump and dark, with a round face with something Asiatic in it. On her head she had a tall kind of red hat.

"That's the Kolta Lapp head-dress," my wife whispered. "I asked her to put it on to show you."

Later, after we had finished the tea and Fetsi had gone to bed, my wife told me more about her.

"She comes from Sevettijärvi."

"Where's Sevettijärvi?" I asked. "And what is a Kolta Lapp?"

"The Swedes call them Skolt Lapps. The Lapps aren't all alike, you know."

I didn't know, and seen from a distance, from England, Lapland had looked as though it would be one country filled with one sort of people—different from England, but homogeneous. Now, surrounded by its vastness, it was becoming increasingly clear that there was room here for many kinds of people, some of whom might be quite different from each other.

"It takes her two and a half days to get home," Arja said. "There isn't any proper road to Sevettijärvi. You have to go up the lakes in summer, though it is a bit easier in winter when you can go over the snow. Some parts of the year it's cut off for a month or so and you can't get there at all."

"How are they different from the other Lapps?"

"They speak a different language and they live in a different sort of place. They're supposed to be very good reindeer men. That's how they make their living—that and fishing."

"Can Fetsi drive a reindeer?"

"Yes," said my wife.

I had never expected that my daughter's first nurse would be able to drive reindeer. I wondered what odd skills and talents Lilian was going to acquire. It was late, however, and time to go to bed. The bedroom was pleasantly warm, in fact the whole of the flat had a comfortable, draughtless feel. It was easy enough inside. But outside? I glanced through the window at the thermometer nailed on the exterior wall. It read minus 30° Centigrade. I had never before seen a thermometer that went down so low. In London, a day or two previously, the temperature had been plus 15. We were cut off from those fierce conditions by a couple of panes of glass and a few inches of woodwork. Easy inside, hard out, I thought: and yet when one meets the hardness one also finds help. It isn't in every place that one so readily encounters the man who moves over to give you a warmer place or who works all night for the public good for nothing, or the heavy gang that won't take any payment.

It was late when I woke in the morning and Fetsi was already preparing coffee in the kitchen. All the lights were on. About nine o'clock I pulled the curtains and looked out. It was still little more than night. Snow stretched out across the fields, over the road, hung in the trees, covered the roofs and disappeared unbroken into the distance. But it was not white snow: the landscape was washed with violet and purple. "Amethyst" is an old word for describing the dawn, though few writers who have used it have been able to get up as late as nine o'clock and see what they described; but there was in that light an extraordinary pureness and clarity which made it peculiarly jewel-like. It came not only from the sky, but also from the ground. The whole atmosphere was filled with the faint but penetrating luminescence, the bare twigs of the trees standing out against it in a thin spidery web. I turned to the other window: low in the extreme south was a lightening of the darkness which was to increase till at mid-day it became a subdued golden glow, the brief reflection of the hidden sun.

A few moments later I put my head inside the surgery door and saw the remaining member of our establishment—Alli Junttila, who came during the day to act as a dental nurse. She was quite unexpectedly good looking and so smartly dressed that my first thought was that she must be on the way out to some bigger place and wouldn't be with us long. In fact she stayed over a year; and I found out later that she belonged to a family which had members throughout Lapland and were known as "the fine Junttilas" because of their accomplished way of dressing.

That morning, however, the dental surgery was not operating, and Arja and I went out to have a look round. The main road continued past our house, and on each side of it were substantial wooden buildings. They rose straight out of the snow, each an individual looking as though it had been placed in the middle of an empty white space with no reference to its neighbours. There were hardly any dividing marks between them. Two or three minutes' walk down the road there was a signpost and a crossroads. The right-hand road went to the Russian border; the left to the hospital; straight ahead there was a long new metal bridge across a river. The bridge carried the road to Norway. On the far side of the river there was a church and some more houses going along towards the east. After that there was nothing except the rippling line of hills which ran round the whole horizon.

The place looked pretty busy. The men we passed either wore fur coats and hats like pillboxes, or short thick jackets and fur-lined caps with big earflaps. I still hadn't got a proper hat—proper in the Lapland sense—and was wearing a flying helmet bought from a surplus stores. I didn't feel too cold but found that breathing had become difficult. People from the American continent and many parts of Europe have some experience of these temperatures but to an Englishman they are a completely new experience and it takes some time to accustom oneself to them. After ten minutes my respiratory system decided that it had done enough accustoming for that day. I said modestly:

"That's enough for now. It's no use trying to see everything the first day. Let's go home."

Before we turned, however, I had seen something which was to become for me a symbol of Lapland. It was a pile of bricks in an empty yard, the remains of a ruined chimney. To explain that pile of blackened bricks I had to find out something of the history of Lapland; and I found also that there is not one Lapland, but two.

3 : *The Bright Lights of Ivalo*

"Heaven's Light Our Guide"

Motto of the
City of Portsmouth

THE summer in Lapland is short, and the winter long: the breath of autumn is sometimes in the air already in August and ice is still on the lakes in June. That first winter, however, never seemed to drag: there was too much that was new to be investigated, and too much human action and interest in the circles in which life ran.

There were three of these. The first was our home, centred round Lilian and the dental surgery, through which passed a constant flow of all types of people; the second was the social intercourse of Ivalo, which surrounded it; and round that again, but much further distant, was the circle which represented the wide, wide world. That was a remote circle which did not affect us greatly and at times it felt as though we might be right outside it, as though we had got disconnected altogether.

As an offset to the length of the winter was the warmth of the home. Outside it was minus thirty, inside plus twenty. There was a sharp rise of fifty degrees Centigrade as one walked through the door. I had never spent such a warm winter before —and all this without lifting a finger. The flat was warmed from the house below by a caretaker who carried out his duty conscientiously. Occasionally, however, a fit of melancholy would come over him in which he wanted to be alone; he then retired to the only place where privacy was possible, the cellar, where he would sit in front of the boiler gloomily throwing logs into it. At those times the temperature of our flat soared up to a tropical heat.

A week or two after my arrival the weather warmed up. The temperature rose to minus fifteen degrees Centigrade (27 degrees of frost Fahrenheit). Then occurred a shocking event. One day in the early afternoon Fetsi wrapped the three-months-old Lilian up in layers of clothes till she looked like a little mummy, and put her in a sleeping bag in her pram. Then she pushed the pram and Lilian outside and left them.

I went to see Arja.

27

"Fetsi's put Lilian outside."

"Well, why not?"

"But there's fifteen degrees of frost. Twenty-seven if you work in Fahrenheit. She'll freeze to death. She's only a tiny baby."

"She won't freeze to death at all. She's been going out ever since we came. It says in the book that you can keep a baby out down to minus fifteen or even minus twenty."

"Not in my book. My book wouldn't dream of leaving a baby out at those temperatures. *It* says: 'Leave the window open at night, wet or fine, in summer and in winter.' "

"If you leave the window open at night we shall all freeze to death—and annoy the caretaker because he'll have to do a lot more heating. She'll be all right. You'll see."

To most parents the first child is something of an experiment. One doesn't know what to do or how to do it. There is, however, as a guide the vaguely remembered experience of one's own youth. Change the environment, and that is gone. In those Arctic surroundings my own experience was no use at all. The rules seemed to have been turned inside out.

However, on that particular day after half an hour there was a healthy yell from outside and Fetsi brought Lilian in, fully alive, very voluble, and extremely hungry. She seemed to have experienced no ill effects due to the cold; nor did she during the whole time we were in Lapland.

Lilian went out during the lightest part of the day, around one o'clock. Only an hour or two separated it from the darkest. At four o'clock night covered the land. The sun had sunk so far below the southern sky that no trace even of its reflection could be seen, and the moon had not yet risen. It was the cold and terrifying moment of desertion when the Universe turned its back on us; and Ivalo floated like a golden bubble on an ocean of darkness, anchored only by the slender cord of the road and the even more fragile threads which ran for ten miles through the forest from the tiny hydro-electric power station.

If the land was dark at four o'clock, at eight o'clock or at midnight it was light again. We would often walk out at night, the hard snow moaning under our ski boots, past the marble houses and the crisp, bright, snow-covered trees. On many nights above our heads there would be great swirls of creamy colour, the aurora, transforming itself from long searchlight beams into single and double arcs right across the centre of the sky, fading into patches and cones until—after minutes or hours—it finally disappeared.

The manifestations of the aurora were varied; but the moon changed its whole character in a single night. It pulled itself slowly up over the northern sky, a huge orange balloon with scarcely enough lift to be airborne. Five hours later it was high overhead and directly above us—or even south—a pure, silvery sphere, the passionless priestess of the skies from whom no corner of the sharp clear landscape could be hidden. Light came from the sky and the snowy earth, from every leaf on every tree. Nothing, it seemed, could remain in darkness. Such a night of truth might follow the day of Judgment. As morning came one looked out again; the priestess had vanished; instead a big bloated old night rake was staggering home towards the north pole.

I rapidly became accustomed to the cold; the greatest inconvenience was the deposit of ice which formed on glasses on going out and the mist on coming in. I quickly picked up know-how about dressing: ski boots and ski trousers, long pants and the fur coat did most of the work, and on all but the very coldest days it was not necessary to wear a pullover. From the waist up I might have been in England—apart, that is to say, from the headgear. Under pressure from my wife I had put the flying-helmet aside and bought a fur hat at Taka Lappi.

Taka Lappi—which means "back Lapland"—and Osuus-kauppa were the two biggest shops in Ivalo, though by no means the only ones. There were few things they did not sell. From a button to a bicycle, from a kilo of butter to a motorized saw—these shops had them; and what they did not have in stock they would order. Of course, the ordering took time; it might be weeks before a major article arrived; but it invariably came, and in the waiting period one had to console oneself with the saying: No hurry in Lapland. But what a wonderful saying it was! All my life there had been hurry. Hurry to be in time for school; hurry to pass examinations at the earliest possible age; hurry to get to work; hurry to catch trains; hurry to keep up with the flood of new knowledge. All the time I had thought this hurry a virtue; and now, suddenly, I realized that it might not be. There could be a different way of living: No hurry in Lapland.

In a small community a shop becomes something of a social centre. At first their interiors were a pattern of dark and light, the heavy browns and blacks in which the customers were dressed contrasting with the white uniforms behind the counter. Then, as we got to know more and more people, the sombre colours receded and in their place the shop was filled with familiar faces. The first person whose face appeared out of the background like this was Maija Saarelainen, wife of *kunnan-johtaja* Eetu Saarelainen, with whom Arja had stayed when she first arrived.

The commune, or administrative district of Inari, in which we were living, had an area of more than 5,000 square miles—about the size of Yorkshire; it was Finland's biggest commune, and in it there were only 6,000 people. Its administration was carried on by an elected council of twenty-one members; Eetu was the chief executive officer of this council. He was an important person in our lives, for he dealt with the arrangements which the commune made with its dentist. Some said he was a difficult man to deal with: we never found him so. As an official and as a friend he did everything possible to introduce us to the life in Inari commune and to make us feel at home with it. His was the first house to which Arja and Lilian went when they first arrived, and it was with the Saarelainens that we spent our last night in Lapland.

Eetu and Maija lived in a three-roomed flat in the *kunnan-talo*—a new building standing by itself which housed the administrative offices of Inari commune and two or three families of those who worked there. The Saarelainens' flat was immaculate; the neat lines of the furniture standing out on the spotless floor gave the impression that all inessentials and impurities had been done away with, that what remained was necessary and spotless and economical.

The rigidity of this well-organized background was broken by two things. One was the flood of green which swept round the room, the plants which Maija so carefully tended. Such indoor gardens are deeply loved in Finland, perhaps because it is, for much of the year, difficult to grow flowers outside. Amongst our friends in Lapland there was a particular preference for cacti, of the sort which—very rarely—flowered. The strange spiky organism, so far from its natural habitat, would be tended carefully through long months until finally it burst into eagerly awaited flowering; then the telephone would ring round Ivalo, and friends would hurry to visit the cactus and offer their congratulations.

The other factor was Eetu himself. Normally he wore a dark office suit, or, outside, the standard winter clothing; but sometimes, when we went to see them on Saturday afternoon, he looked quite different. He would be sitting, relaxed, with the dark winter jacket gone and instead a yellow shirt, worn American style, with gay pictures on it. There was somewhere in Eetu a deep colourful streak, hidden most of the time but ready to make its way out when given the opportunity.

Maija and Eetu had lived much further north. Formerly this north-eastern arm of Finland ran right up to the Arctic Ocean. The main road from Rovaniemi turned right at Ivalo and ran on till it reached the town of Petsamo at the end of this arm. Eetu had worked in the administration of Petsamo.

"Weren't you cold up there?" I asked once, thinking that a hundred miles further north than Ivalo must be rather frozen.

He shook his head. "No. It was much warmer in Petsamo than it is here. The winters were shorter."

The statistics supported him; the February temperature of the coast of the Arctic Ocean near Petsamo is at least ten degrees warmer than Ivalo. The days in Petsamo were cut short. In November 1939 war broke out between Russia and Finland, and the Russians advanced into the Petsamo area. This was the so-called "winter war" with Russia, a war in which it looked at first as though Finland would be crushed in a few weeks. The unexpectedly stubborn and united resistance of the Finns turned the war into a protracted and terrible struggle in a winter so cold that lower temperatures had only been recorded twice in the last hundred years.

However gallant the struggle, the Finns could not prolong it indefinitely; it ended in the Peace of Moscow in March 1940. The Peace took from Finland a large slice of territory in the south, but still left the outlet to the sea through Petsamo in Finnish hands.

This was, however, only the overture. Trapped between opposing powers, and doubtful of the intentions of her overwhelmingly strong Russian neighbour, Finland could not afford to refuse a German request for transit facilities through Finland to Norway. Germany and Russia were in any case at that time ostensibly good friends. With the waning of this friendship, Finland became in an increasingly difficult position. When Germany attacked Russia it was not possible for Finland, with German forces on her soil, to remain outside the conflict, and once again Finland was at war with Russia.

Ironically, before peace came, Finland had been at war not only with Russia, but also with Germany. When the fortunes of war swung away from Germany, Finland signed an armistice in 1944 which stipulated that all German forces must be removed by a given date.

The Germans, who resisted, were driven out by force. The majority of them were stationed in Lapland. As they went they set fire to every house along the road, blew up every bridge, destroyed the boats and cut the fishing nets. Out of 2,000 buildings in Rovaniemi, only a hundred were left and along the road nothing remained standing but blackened chimney bricks, of the sort I had seen that first day in Ivalo. Lapland, a United Nations observer said later, was more completely destroyed than any other part of Europe.

The region, some said, had suffered so much that it should be abandoned: it could not be re-made for twenty years. But the obstinate people of Lapland went back as soon as the last German soldiers had been expelled: back to the scorched and blackened fields, the burnt forests, and the race against the rapidly approaching bitter cold. During that first winter those without houses lived in the trenches left over from the war; but the country was rapidly rebuilt. It was, however, like death and resurrection: the villages and towns were still in the same position on the map, but they had been created anew: new homes, new shops, new schools. It was unusual to see any building which was more than a few years old; and yet, mingling with this modernity were ways of life which went back to the days before the wheel was invented.

Not all those who went back to Lapland could return even to the patch of ground on which their home had formerly stood. By the Peace Treaty of 1947 Finland had been compelled to give up her outlet to the Arctic Ocean, the province of Petsamo. The road which had formerly turned right at Ivalo and gone on north and west till it reached the coast, was cut; the border ran across it at Virtaniemi, thirty miles east of Ivalo. Many of those who had formerly lived in Petsamo went instead to the most northerly remaining communes of Finnish Lapland. Such were the Saarelainens.

Another very well-known man in Ivalo who had also been in Petsamo was Kalle. It is wrong, perhaps, to introduce him as "Kalle"; I knew him first as the *nimismies*, or sheriff; but it was as "Kalle" or "*nimis*-Kalle" that he was universally known throughout the commune of Inari. Anyone talking about "the sheriff" was almost certainly a foreigner and no true member of Ivalo society.

"*Nimismies*" translated literally means "names-man" since in earlier days one of the principal tasks of the *nimismies* was the record of the inhabitants. It is usually translated into English as "sheriff". To anyone brought up in an English industrial County Borough, "sheriff" is an obscure term. It conveys an impression of a remote figure appointed by the Crown, of some social standing and vague powers, the sheriff of the English county; mixed with this is a more colourful picture from American films, the hard-bitten sheriff of the Wild West,

bursting violently into the saloon and shooting up the local
bad hats; and in the background is a distant memory of Robin
Hood and the Wicked Sheriff of Nottingham.

It was with great interest, therefore, that I learnt one day
that we were to give a small coffee party at which the *nimismies*
and his wife would be present. Which of my three pictures
would he most closely resemble?

In fact, he didn't resemble any of them: he didn't arrive at
all. At half past ten his wife, Sirkka, who had come, said: "I'm
sorry. I'm afraid Kalle must have fallen asleep in the *sauna*."
This, it transpired later, was exactly what had happened: and
it was really our fault for issuing an invitation on a night which
was by tradition devoted to the *sauna*, or steam bath. So my
cloudy picture of the *nimismies* remained unresolved. It
was left in that state until we went to a dinner-dance at
Maja.

Maja was a building close by the Ivalo crossroads. It was
owned by the Finnish Tourist Association and in summer was
principally a hotel for travellers. In winter a large part of the
organized social life of Ivalo centred round it. On its ground
floor Maja had two main public rooms, both restaurants, but of
different class. The one to the left of the main entrance was the
cheaper and simpler one; the one straight ahead was more
elaborately furnished and in summer had a pleasant view of
the river. Dancing took place in the hall, a no-man's-land
between the two restaurants, and also invaded the less
expensive one.

As we were on the point of leaving, my wife suddenly said,
"There's the *nimismies*."

He came to our table; no guns in the holster, no formality,
just a suggestion that he knew his way around, and a face with
significant lines on it—the broad right-to-left lines that come
from an expression which laughs more than it frowns. He
wanted to know if I would have a drink. Thank you, I said,
but we were just going. Have some of mine, at least, he said,
and offered me the other side of his glass.

Then the conversation lagged. Kalle, like most men over
forty in Finland, spoke German but not much English; my
knowledge of Finnish was very rudimentary, and my German
not fluent enough to achieve a real meeting of minds. Finnish,
English, and German all being inadequate, what was left?
Latin, obviously, thought Kalle.

"*In vino veritas*," he said, raising his glass towards me.

"*Dum spiro spero*," I replied, not to be outdone.

"*Sic transit gloria mundi*," and Kalle drained his glass.

We left shortly afterwards. "The *nimismies* seems a very informal sort of man," I said to my wife as I pulled the fur collar of my overcoat up over my ears.

"He is," she said. "But he's right for the people here."

The presence of crime has a more marked effect than its absence. It was only later when I came back from Lapland and found my friends carefully locking their doors at night that I realized how little crime there had been in Inari commune. We did, it is true, usually lock the door when we went to bed; but if we didn't remember in time, no one bothered to get up. There was very little theft, and few crimes of violence. I once left a suitcase unlocked and unattended for half an hour in the centre of Ivalo by the roadside without worrying at all as to whether it would be there when I came back.

But what of the Lapps? I had been a week or two in Ivalo without seeing any traces of them when suddenly one afternoon when the short-lived daylight had almost disappeared I noticed a strange-looking creature standing by the side of the road in the main street. I couldn't make out what it was at first; then it moved its head, and I saw a pair of horns which looked, in the twilight, gigantic. A reindeer. There was a low dark shape on the ground behind it, and as I watched a man came rushing out of the shop, his strange cornered head-gear standing out for a second against the sky. He hurled himself towards the dark shape and instantly the whole outfit took off with the acceleration of a sports car.

Then one day my wife came into the room in which I was working.

"Have a look in the waiting room," she said.

I went down the corridor to the small room which served jointly as entrance hall for us and waiting room for the surgery. It had become suddenly colourful as though an exotic plant had all at once burst into flower—a brilliant display of red and yellow and blue. There were three of them—Lapp father, mother and little Lapp boy not yet old enough to stand by himself. The woman wore a dark blue dress, with bright stripes of red and yellow bounding its lower edge, its sleeves, and running down from its shoulder; it was held at the waist by a white belt figured in red. On her shoulders was a white tasselled shawl.

The man wore a skirt-like garment, similarly coloured, which finished around his knees; below that were ample blue trousers running into reindeer-skin boots, with their turned-up toes. Near him was the "cap of the four winds", with its circular base and above the soft blue material drawn into four points which drooped gently towards the four corners of the sky. The boy was a small replica of the man.

People can't walk round on their ordinary business dressed like that. This must be some kind of stage show—that was my first reaction to Lappish clothing. My second was directly opposite; why is our own clothing so unattractive? At the end of a long process of evolution and industrial development we reach its most noble product—as we think—Western man; and we dress him in colours so drab and uninteresting, so utterly dreary, that an unbiassed observer from another planet would surely conclude that we were secretly ashamed of him.

Not all Lapps, however, dressed like this: at least, not on weekdays. The real Lappish costume was often a best suit worn on special occasions and for visits to the capital of the commune—Ivalo. These were the people who lived the most truly Lappish life, having their homes in isolated wooden houses by some lakeside far from the road, and only coming into Ivalo occasionally. But there were also other Lapps who lived in and around Ivalo, who had ordinary regular work, and who would not have appeared to an outsider any different from the rest of the Ivalo population. To complicate the situation further, Finns who had lived in Lapland for a few years frequently bought a Lapp costume and wore it on suitable occasions.

It would, therefore, be quite possible for a tourist to go through Lapland without seeing a single Lapp, and on greeting the first person he saw in Lappish costume, to find he was talking to the Sodankylä dentist or the Utsjoki policeman.

But who are the Lapps? Finnish children are taught at school that the Lapps are of a different race but speak a language related to Finnish. They were in Finland before the Finns and originally spread out through the whole country. Through the centuries they have been pushed north until in Finland they are only found well north of the Arctic Circle. Lapland is in some respects like a colony: the Finns, both those who have been born there and those who each year move in to Lapland, usually live in towns and villages along the road, whilst the Lapps who most truly retain their original character retreat as far as possible into the wilderness.

So there are two Laplands: the Lapland of the roads and towns, and the Lapland of the wilds.

The picture is not simple. Different groups of Lapps live in different ways; some marry Finns and adopt Finnish ways; some Finns to a limited extent adopt Lappish ways of life.

One more surprise was waiting for me in Ivalo. The

telephone rang one evening; Arja came back from answering it with a peculiar smile on her face.

"That was from Russia." Her tone was provocative.

"Russia? Do we actually get phone calls from Russia here? Who was it?"

"A patient."

"Can they cross the border then?"

"Oh yes. They're Finns, not Russians, and in a way they don't feel as though they were in Russia because all that area belonged to Finland before the war."

"But what are they doing?"

"They're building a power station. There's a lot of water power over there, at Rajakoski. That's one reason why the Russians wanted it and why this commune is poorer than it would otherwise be. They gave the contract for building it to the Finns. The Rajakoski people often come in on a Saturday afternoon; I'm the nearest dentist."

After a while I accepted the Rajakoski people from Russia and the Lapps from the wilderness as perfectly natural phenomena. Our establishment was compressed, however; the bathroom opened directly off the entrance hall, which was also the waiting room; and it still disconcerted me when going there in the morning to be greeted by a row of little schoolgirl patients, curtseying respectfully.

4 : Reindeer and Ski-ing

"And then, and then came spring, and rose-in-hand . . ."

SPRING came; not rose-in-hand, but accompanied by something better than roses—indeed, the source of all springs and
all roses—the sun. The sun leapt up into the sky with no false
diffidence or modesty, but with gay exuberance as though it
were coming back to its rightful kingdom. Each day the dark
hours shrank perceptibly until one morning Arja said: "We're
passing them now." By "them" she meant the rest of the world
south of the Arctic Circle, the people who had seen light
throughout the winter whilst we had lain in a great darkness.
But now our turn had come; the universe was dissolving and
changing, and from then on the sun was to be ours, more and
more—lingering every day longer until finally he could not
leave us at all but hung devotedly even in the midnight sky.
Dissolve: that is precisely what happened to the landscape.
The thick piles of snow by the side of the road softened and
melted, turning themselves into uncountable rivulets which
trickled into the ditches and across the highway. Tears appeared on the white smooth sheet on which we had been living;
patches of dark mongrel-coloured earth as the fields slowly
came out of hibernation, slushy muck where the fundamental
surface of the road revealed itself, unexpected fences and paths
which had been hidden so deeply that one never suspected
their existence. The snow dropped off the trees and they stood
in dark lines on the hills, ringing us round in a complete circle.
But before this change had taken place, when the sun was
in the sky but whilst the snow was still hard and smooth and
the skis ran easily over it, came one of the peak periods of the
year when life was especially colourful and characteristic: late
February, March and early April, when the reindeer round-
ups were reaching their climax and ski-ing was at its best.
We went first to a round-up which was fifteen miles away,
on a dull day before spring had progressed very far. A taxi
took us along the main road, which was fairly wide, then turned
down a side road which looked much too narrow to hold anything beyond our own vehicle, if that. It was a lonely way, winding between the hills, with scarcely a hut to show that the region
was inhabited. We did, finally, meet another car coming in the

opposite direction; both drivers philosophically shovelled snow away till there was room to squeeze by. We reached the nearest point to the round-up, walked across the snow, and came to a fence. We climbed the fence and were in the active area.

A short distance away a big crowd of brown and grey reindeer were peacefully nosing in the snow for the moss which they eat. Tethered to a tree was the leader, the bell round its neck making a musical metallic note as the creature moved its head. The reindeer were inside a very large enclosed space; a fence ran round this, and at its end was a small central enclosure with several ways opening out of it. A few men were standing inside this; some had part Lappish dress, most looked as though they had their old clothes on. (Well, wouldn't you?) The sun looked out from behind the clouds for a minute and shone down peacefully on the quiet scene.

A man walked out to the bell reindeer, untethered it, and began to lead it towards the central enclosure. The noise increased as he came nearer to us, the rhythmic clanging seeming like the prelude to some dramatic rite. He walked through into the central enclosure; some of the reindeer followed and the gates were shut.

Peace vanished. There was a frantic trampling of hooves, a wild rush of reindeer round the impenetrable circle in which they were trapped, and a swaying, tumbling confusion as the reindeer fought for freedom and man fought for his lordship over nature. A dozen separate fights were going on between man and animal; the reindeer owners, each looking for his own beasts, seized the animals by the horns, by the leg, by whatever they could take hold of, and pushed, pulled, or even half carried their reluctant property through the gate into the owner's section.

It did not last long. In a few moments the last of the reindeer had been flung into its proper place, the men were resting and the sun was still shining peacefully on the quiet scene as the other reindeer ate tranquilly.

The reindeer was originally a wild creature, roaming over the hills at its will, and hunted by man for the food and clothing it could give him. But it is also a draught animal; a man in a sledge behind one can travel over the hard snow more rapidly than by any other form of non-mechanical transport. Men began to keep draught reindeer and the herds increased in size until now there are in Finland no wild reindeer. Each has its owner, who puts his characteristic mark on its ear. To hunt or kill a reindeer of which one is not the owner is direct stealing.

Man has, however, only partially tamed this creature. It never looks at him with the worshipping eyes of a dog, or even with the contented acceptance of the horse. It watches man to see if he is watching it, and if man's attention is wandering the reindeer will be off on its own concerns. A horse acting on its own responsibility might bring its master home; a reindeer would probably take him into the wilderness.

The purpose of the round-up is to mark the reindeer born that year, to count them (there is a tax to be paid for each reindeer owned), to castrate some, and to kill others. Castration is sometimes carried out by the teeth; I was told that in the low temperatures prevalent this was less likely to harm the animal than using a knife. The Lapps are wonderfully adept at recognizing their own earmarks, even though there are some thousands in existence, and in quickly cutting these on the ear of the reindeer.

Poetic though it looks at times, the round-up is also a vast open-air slaughter house. There may be thousands of reindeer in one of the bigger round-ups, which will go on for days or even weeks; and hundreds will be killed. The round-up is also a sales organization: meat buyers from Rovaniemi and other towns are there to purchase wholesale quantities of reindeer meat.

A reindeer can provide a very high proportion of the things which a Lapp family needs: food; transport; clothing from its hide; underclothing from the soft skins of baby reindeer; shoes; even thread for sewing. Nowadays, however, there is a tendency for the Lapps to buy more from the towns and make less for themselves. A reindeer owner would keep some draught reindeer for transport, would put aside some reindeer meat for his own consumption from amongst the animals that were killed, and would sell the rest.

Reindeer skins were hung outside throughout the winter when taken from the reindeer; after this they could be made into clothing or rugs.

In spring the reindeer are released and move upward to their summer feeding grounds, with herdsmen following and trying to keep the herd together. Through the summer they wander farther and farther away until in autumn the great return begins. The reindeer men begin to gather the animals together again; first the scattered stragglers are gathered together in small groups, then the groups join together and the increasing number move slowly towards their destination —the fence inside which the sorting and marking is to take place.

Throughout the autumn and winter and on into the spring this goes on. Some of the reindeer fences are near to the reindeer herds, and here the round-ups take place first, sometimes already in autumn; but the more distant reindeer do not reach their destination until the next spring. Those not killed or kept for draught purposes are set free to wander through the cycle of the seasons once again.

In earlier days the movement was much greater, the reindeer going up to the shores of the Arctic Ocean in summertime. In those days the Lapps were truly nomadic, living in the typical tent with a hole in the top, supported by three branches. But times changed. In 1852 the Finnish–Norwegian border was closed, and movement was no longer so free. Around 1900 the Lapps began increasingly to build fixed wooden houses instead of tents and now these are almost universal. There are in Finland hardly any true nomads left. Most people in Lapland live in houses, many in their own houses.

And yet—and yet—there was a difference between the reindeer men we knew in Inari commune (even the Finnish ones) and our friends in England. My friends in England do not usually disappear for three months each year, sleeping out at night as they move with the reindeer herds, and occasionally ski-ing for twenty miles to ring up their wives and say they are all right. The true nomads have disappeared, but Lapland life is still not enclosed throughout the year in four walls.

On Marianpäiva—Lady Day—there was a yearly gathering of the Lapps, first for service in the church in the village of Inari, later for the reindeer races. This was the new church, set in trees between the village and the lake. It was the first church in which I had seen paintings of reindeer on the walls. In the middle was a sea of rippling red—the fluttering caps of the Lappish girls. They startled the eye; the Finnish Lutheran State church is normally filled with sad sombre shades. The girls seemed to have innocently introduced an essential gaiety which others had forgotten.

The blue and red figures surged out of the church and into the nearby eating places. These were quickly crowded to overflowing and filled with smoke and the peculiar sound of mixed Lappish and Finnish. Then the sports began. First was the lassooing, in which the competitors tried to throw the rope noose over a stick on the far side of a circle. It was an intimate gathering; both men and girls were competing and advice and comments were shouted out freely.

Then the crowd broke away from the circle and arranged itself for the reindeer races. They were held on the frozen surface of the lake, on which a track had been cleared; the banks round its sides provided a natural amphitheatre which could have accommodated a cup-final crowd with ease. Reindeer, tethered, were grazing at the top of the bank, and at intervals men leading the animals pushed their way down the steep slope to the lake and joined the knot of organizers and competitors at the beginning of the track.

"They're off!" Not they, but he: one man on skis pulled by his reindeer, and urging it on—almost disappearing from sight round the far end of the great circle—growing larger and larger as he flew towards the finishing line—then the crowd scattering as man and reindeer shot off the course and pulled themselves up on the steep lake side.

It was an entirely individual affair, and after having been seen a few times became less interesting except when someone fell into the snow. After some time we decided to go back. The roads at this time of the year were at their most treacherous. The taxi drivers were highly skilled drivers who knew exactly how fast they could go; but the surface was so slippery that the taxi skidded a little at each corner for twenty-five miles: never very much, just enough to remind us on what an insecure basis life rested.

I was, however, during that spring, struggling with another problem: ski-ing. Everyone in Lapland skis. Small boys rush down precipitous hills, apparently dangerously out of control; at the height of their speed they see a friend and by what looks like some supernatural means, stop dead. The President of Finland comes, every year, to Lapland for a ski-ing holiday. The reindeer men ski hundreds and thousands of kilometres after the reindeer. There are ski-ing competitions for children, with a special class for those under four. It is the universal sport.

But I did not ski. I had to learn.

One night Arja, with her friend Eila Erola, the head of the high school, took me out to an inconspicuous part of the river bank just behind the Taka Lappi stores. They lashed skis on my feet and gave me a gentle push.

Up to that moment there had been foolish pictures in my mind: dreams that ski-ing would be the art which I had never tried, yet for which I had an undoubted natural talent; that I should glide along masterfully whilst the bystanders called out: "Surely you must have done this before!"

It wasn't at all like that. I travelled along, very slowly, for about half a yard; then the ground dipped downwards abruptly, my velocity increased uncontrollably, and I sat down. That, for many many times, was the pattern of my efforts:

DETERMINATION – CONSTERNATION – FRUSTRATION.

Lapland is an inspiring place in which to ski; but it is not, perhaps, the best place in which to learn to ski, since it is not assumed that anyone will need teaching. My own training was on a little hill at the back of the house in which we lived. I stood at the top, pushed off, and went down to the bottom, hoping to remain upright and trying at least to land on a different part of the body each time. It was sometimes a relief when darkness made it possible to retire inside without dishonour. Occasionally a group of Lapland boys would watch me. They made no offensive remarks; they simply stared blankly as though they could not possibly comprehend how any adult could behave like that.

It was, really, not the best way to learn ski-ing; proper lessons at the beginning from a ski instructor might have saved much time and unnecessary discomfort. But in the end I gained a dubious sense of balance and some idea as to how to limit the speed reached. Turning was still a mysterious and incomprehensible art.

Ski-ing in Finnish Lapland has its own characteristics. It is not, usually, mountain ski-ing. In the north-west, near Kilpisjärvi, there are mountains rising to over four thousand feet; the other heights are rounded hills mostly under half that height. The tops of these hills—*tunturit*—are bare; but the tree line is soon reached and the ski tracks slip down between the trees. It is at long-distance ski-ing, needing great powers of endurance, through this sort of rolling, wooded country, that the Finns are expert. The beginner, confronted simultaneously with a steep slope, a right-angle bend, and a tree, cannot help wishing that he were free to study each of these problems separately.

The other quality which Finnish Lapland ski-ing possesses is that it is so readily available. It is no luxury sport. In any spare hour one can start off from one's own back door and in a few moments be surrounded by the white slopes and the uncountable trees. One may without difficulty go for several hours seeing no other human being and hearing nothing except the swish of the wood on the snow.

After much practice I at last became sufficiently stable on the skis to make my first infant's progress into the woods, and one Sunday Arja took me out.

"Don't be so stiff!" she called out to me. "Bend your legs!"

I slunk obediently after her, down the road till we reached

the hut owned by the ski club, then into the sunlit forest, a pattern of clear gold and frozen green. The ski club were having a competition that day; as we went along the trail from time to time a voice from behind would shout out "Hup!" and a blue-clad figure with a white cap with a knob on it would fly by. I stared at these high-velocity figures with something of the same expression with which the Wright's biplane might stare at a transatlantic jet. Could such things really be possible?

Arja led me to the edge of a precipice. It upset me to see her so near the edge; I hurried up to warn her, but before I could get there she calmly shot off down it on her skis.

"Come on," she called out to me from the bottom. I hesitated. "What are you waiting for?" There was a note of righteous impatience in her voice. "Put your feet together in a V and come down like that. You can't go too fast then."

I moved my feet into a clumsy V. It didn't seem very effective.

"All right," she shouted finally. "If you can't do that then come down sideways."

I crawled down the slippery slope like a crab on an iceberg and arrived somewhat ruffled at the bottom. There are many things one can find in Lapland, and one or two one can lose. Dignity is one of them.

On any fine day—and most days in the spring were fine, flooded with sunshine and keen pure air—the creamy tops of the hills beckoned over the woods below them. It was quite possible to reach some of these directly from Ivalo; but the real Mecca of the ski-ers was Kaunispää. The *Saariseläntunturit* are a range of low mountains running east-west across Finnish Lapland and cutting the main Rovaniemi road about fifteen miles south of Ivalo. They are a watershed, the rivers to the north of Saariselkä draining into the Arctic Ocean and those south reaching the Gulf of Bothnia. Kaunispää—which means literally "beautiful head"—is the name of the *tunturi* over which the main road runs.

On fine Sundays in the ski-ing season the buses to Kaunispää and from it were crowded with skis, ski sticks, and their owners. Since there were only four buses a day, it was no joke to miss the bus back and have to wait till the small hours of the morning to return. The more fortunate strapped their skis like lances on the top of motor transport. We were lucky enough to have friends in Jaakko, the commune secretary, and Liisi, his attractive wife, who owned a Volkswagen. Jaakko, who was much bigger than the average Finn, almost reached to the roof of the Volkswagen. One Sunday he and Liisi drove round and we all went off to Kaunispää.

Kaunispää itself was shaped like the shell of a tortoise, white and smooth on top, with its curved sides sloping down to the trees in the valley below. Round it rose the other *tunturit*, Ahopää opposite, Palopää, Urupää and Kuusipää behind, and in the distance Kiilopää, the tallest of them all. In those days Kaunispää was comparatively undeveloped; on top was the *Ylämaja* or "upper hostel" which provided the most expensive, highest quality service; down in the valleys there were other simpler, cheaper, hostels capable of accommodating more people. (Now Kaunispää has an ultra-high-frequency radio transmitter and a modern hotel is being built.)

Further away from the main road was a hut called *Ruma-kuru* or *Rumakurun kämppä*. It was one of the most accessible of a large number of such huts which are scattered over the trails of Lapland and which provide a free shelter overnight for the traveller. All he need do in return is to sweep the floor and replenish the store of firewood. Rumakuru was, however, so near to the main road that it was used not so much for over-night stays as for mid-day picnics. My memory of that first day at Kaunispää, much though I enjoyed it, is not so much of the excitement of ski-ing or the beauty of the landscape, as of arriving at Rumakuru long after the rest of the party and see-ing Liisi holding up a big circular sausage which she had just cooked over the wood fire. It is a sausage which I shall always remember, eaten to the rhythmic "whump" of virtuoso ski-ers who were coming down the steep hillside behind the *kämppä* and slowing themselves on the opposite slope.

Other people had their own private *kämppäs*. On a later day Eetu, the *kunnanjohtaja*, and his wife Maija, took me to theirs. We drove along the main road northwards for some miles, then unshipped the skis and struck off into the forest. After a couple of hours gentle ski-ing—Eetu was very understanding of the difficulties which some of us were experiencing—we reached a spot in a little valley in which was arranged some seats with a covering over them, some cut wood, and stones on which a fire had obviously been built and on which it was soon blazing again. We sat round it, eating reindeer meat sandwiches; and the rest of the world might have been a thousand miles away or might not have existed at all. I had many reflections on the way back; on the fact that one could leave one's belongings out here for months and not be afraid that anyone would interfere with them; that one could begin ski-ing earlier and continue it later than any other sport I knew; and on the discovery that at last I could turn whilst ski-ing. This gave me great joy, com-parable to that of a child on learning to walk; and, indeed, trying to acquire these new faculties when already adult sharpens one's understanding of the enormous problems children face.

But the climax of that short intense season was our ski-ing holiday—a week which we spent in Kaunispää at Ylämaja. We would set out in the morning, gliding over the smooth top of the *tunturi* and after that taking a different direction each day. We had a little kettle and some food, and when we were hungry lit a fire from pieces of dry wood which we picked up, and suspended the kettle above it on a long, forked stick. Water was obtained by putting lumps of snow into the kettle, for which it seemed to have a huge appetite. After a little while we would knock the fire out and move on, and there would be a trace of sadness in doing so—as though one had created a home and were now destroying it. Perhaps that is the penalty in being a nomad with a longing for home, a wanderer with a desire for stability, that whether one goes or stays one must always feel that pang of nostalgia for the other.

In the evening we would climb slowly back up the hill to the meal which Ylämaja had ready for us, and then, after a glance at the travel literature in the rack, and a re-examination of the map to find where we really had been, we would go up to our room. It was an extraordinary little room, in a tiny tower at one end of Ylämaja. It had four windows, one on each side; from it one could look out in all directions as though one were in command of the landscape. It had its lighthearted moods and its more frightening ones. One evening a snow storm blew up the hill and the snowflakes whirled round the tower till it seemed to have floated off the earth altogether and to be lost in a sea of snow. But mostly we looked out at a friendly country, clean, and inviting us to come out and play with it for another day.

Our last expedition was to Kiilopää. This could be reached most easily from the road a few miles further down; we took a bus to this point and then went straight into the forest. We ploughed between the trees—the snow was then hard enough to make this not too difficult—up and down through little hollows and valleys till finally we left the trees behind and reached the *tunturi* itself. It was abominably slippery. I could not see how, if by some miracle I reached the top, I could ever get down again. My wife was ahead—she always was in those days—and she called out to me to wait at the bottom if my ski-ing wasn't up to the *tunturi*. If she had been a man of my own nationality I undoubtedly should have done so. She wasn't, so I went on and a long time after her I crawled up to the pile of stones which marked the highest point. It was a magnificent view; line after line of mountains rippled round the horizon and below us the trees trickled like a dark liquid through the valleys.

We got lost on the way back. One rarely knows the exact moment at which one becomes lost; when one finds out one has usually been lost for some time. We were going up a valley when it suddenly struck me forcibly that if we were going in the right direction then the sun was not. After thinking this out carefully I pointed it out to Arja. She agreed, after a moment, and we turned round and went back to the outlet of the valley. We realized that we didn't know very much about where we were and consulted the map. After studying it for some time we decided that the map didn't know very much either: it certainly had no knowledge of the numerous valleys we could see in front of us.

We continued in what seemed the right direction. The country seemed to be cut up by river valley after river valley; each we confidently expected would be the one for which we were looking, which ran from Kaunispää to Rumukuru. Each we climbed out of wearily after it had been proved to be unsatisfactory. Finally we reached a long upsloping tableland, and I began to despair. We came to the edge and looked down into the next valley.

It was not empty. Below in the valley I could see the ski tracks—and I suddenly realized what a dynamic thing a ski track is, and how in such lonely country even the appearance of a ski track makes it look populated. We reached Ylämaja in the last rays of light; we had seen no one but each other all day.

The next year we found the easy way to Kiilopää: a broad track with no difficulties about it at all, and a short and easy way down on which we met quite a number of people. It was easy and simple—but how much better had been that long, lonely mixed-up way through the snow we had taken the year before!

5 : *The Post Path to Utsjoki*

THE white turned to brown, then the brown was washed away by the flood of green which came pouring over the landscape. Nature's scene-shifters work fast in Lapland. As June approached the nights grew shorter than I had ever seen them and finally disappeared altogether. We put up dark paper blinds over the windows to give an illusion of night. In the middle of the month we made an expedition to Utsjoki.

Utsjoki is in the extreme north of Finnish Lapland. It is at the junction of two rivers—the Teno, which flows northwards along the border between Finland and Norway, bends round, and finally reaches the Arctic Ocean; and the Utsjoki, which runs into it. The one word "Utsjoki" is the name of three things: a river, a village, and a commune. The commune is the most lonely and isolated in Finland, and also the one which has the highest proportion of Lappish people. Until 1957 there was no road to the village: it could only be reached by an eight hours' trip up the river or by a sixty-mile walk. At the time we went the new road to Utsjoki was under construction; the last part of it, however, was still unbuilt.

We left Ivalo late one June afternoon, taking the bus which went along the road going northwards. It was a road which I came to know better than any other in Lapland, the main highway to Norway, and Inari, the old centre of the commune. It went over the long, new metal bridge and past the wooden church, over the hill past the ski club's headquarters, the sharp bend on the other side of the hill where the road crossed a little stream, then the woods closed round as Ivalo disappeared from sight. Near the bridge over the stream was a sign which said ominously: Bends for thirty-eight kilometres. That was almost the whole distance to Inari, and between Ivalo and Inari there were no habitations except one or two isolated wooden houses.

A few miles further on the road rose to a sharp bend below which the trees dropped away, then sloped down towards the water. This was not the great lake of Inari itself, but Ukonjärvi, one of the lesser lakes which ran into it. The road went along the edge of the lake for some distance, swerved past the white cube of the power station, and underneath *Karhunpesäkivi*—"The bear's cave stone"—where a man is once reputed to have spent a night with a bear. The stone was hollow, the hollow being shaped like a semicircle so that one could crawl right round. There was plenty of room for both a man and a bear, but it must have been a strange night.

After that the road turned away from the lakes, and ran between the hills till through the trees came once again the shimmer of the sun on the water. This was Inari, as wide as the English Channel and twice as long as it was wide, with some 3,000 islands in it. Here was also the village of Inari, only one-tenth the size of Ivalo, but still conscious that it had been originally the centre of the commune and a little irritated that the once unimportant Ivalo now completely overshadowed it. It retained, however, the distinction of being the "Church-Village"—the village at which the principal church in the district was situated; and when the new church was built, it was built at Inari. Small though Inari was it possessed a good hotel, from the dining room of which one looked out on to the turbulent waters of the Juutuanjoki where it ran into the great lake. We stayed here overnight. We were both tired: the number of patients coming to see Arja had been enormously greater than our expectations, and I had been struggling to get my thesis finished before the University shut up for the summer. Perhaps this tiredness was one of the factors which contributed to the catastrophe we were to meet.

We woke late the next morning and set out by taxi which was to take us as far as the road went. Since bus services were limited and on some roads non-existent, a taxi was frequently the most suitable way of reaching a distant point; the drivers were quite accustomed to being taken off the rank and asked to do a journey of fifty miles. There was a tale that the dentist who was Arja's predecessor in Ivalo had once got into a taxi and said "Stockholm". It was certainly true that tourists sometimes took a taxi straight off the rank for a three-day trip into Norway and back. Taxi driving in Ivalo had a gambler's thrill about it: the next customer might want to go 100 miles or only 100 yards.

The road to Inari is a very old traditional way, which has been followed for centuries; but past Inari it only dates back to the days of the war. Earlier maps show the road proper ending at Inari, and nothing beyond this but footpaths. The old route to the Arctic Ocean was along the eastern side of Lake Inari, to Petsamo; when Petsamo was taken over by the U.S.S.R. at the end of the war the traffic swung over to this western outlet, which is now a motor road running up through Inari and then swinging east through Karigasniemi into Norway, finally reaching the Norwegian Arctic Highway and the Arctic Ocean itself.

The Bacon family outside their home in Ivalo : (left to right) Henry, Arja, Walter and Lilian

Our home in Ivalo

The Council offices, Ivalo

Our taxi followed this road for twenty miles. Although we were 200 miles beyond the Arctic Circle the land was surprisingly rich-looking: forests of birch and pine broken by occasional farms. Just past the small village of Kaamanen the new road to Utsjoki left the main Inari–Karigasniemi road. It was not so broad, and the country was now barer and more sombre: pools and marshes stretched out mysteriously on either side. Suddenly the road rose to the top of a height and the Norwegian mountains appeared in the distance. Thirty miles further on the taxi stopped in a valley, and we got out. On the slopes were two or three long wooden huts: this was the construction camp for the men working on the road, and we were almost at its end. The hills curved gracefully down to a smooth sheet of water with a tree-covered island rising in the middle, and the sun shone from the north directly along the way we were going. The sharp little stones ground under our feet as we left the valley and walked along a ridge, a typically Finnish ridge sloping sharply down to a river on each side. The road descended once more and crossed a bridge—still only partly finished.

There the road ended. It ran through the forest like a dragon, tearing up trees and rocks and spitting them out on either side; but this was the farthest point to which it had been able to eat its way. Beyond lay the peaceful path, a light strip of earth wandering between the friendly trees. There was a clear savage line of demarcation between the road and the forest; but the edges of the path were blurred, as though it had been there so long that it was woven into nature.

This was a post path, the old post path which ran from Kaamanen to Utsjoki. There were several Lappish houses along it; even though so isolated they possessed a regular mail service, the postman coming along the post path either walking or cycling. There were also five *autiotupa*—simple huts with wooden beds and a fireplace in which travellers could stay the night. It would usually take the postman several days to get back to the post office.

We walked steadily along the post path; it was very late in the evening, but in June in Lapland it is more pleasant to travel by night than by day. At midnight we decided we needed some rest; I was beginning to wonder if all the things in the rucksack were really necessary. No elaborate arrangements were required; in the warm, late night we simply went a few yards aside from the path and unrolled our sleeping bags.

I woke early. The microscopic jungle of moss and grasses

under the sleeping bag moved springily as I sat up. It covered the hillside on which we were lying, ash-colour and emerald flecked with red. Below, the river lay still and quiet in the intense sunshine. On the opposite side the trees rose up, dark green and motionless, till they reached the blue backcloth of the sky. It was a moment, not of becoming, but of being; in which the inanimate hills, the life which had grown out of them, and a voice in me cried out that the ultimate triumph and satisfaction was existence itself!

I made some tea over a little fire, stubbing out little trickles of flame that edged away into the moss. Then we walked on. The trees in a Lapland forest are thinner than those in the south, and spaced apart; this, with the colourful ground pattern, gives a strange effect of design. Here, in the most natural landscape in Europe, one feels at times as though one were in a vast ornamental park.

We had not really slept enough, and about eleven o'clock we stopped to make some coffee. Perhaps, if we had been fresher, we should have noticed that we were on a hill and that there was a wind blowing up the hill. Perhaps we should have paid more attention to the dry branches which were heaped up ready to be taken away. Perhaps, if I had not been cautious and pessimistic, I should not have been so careful to make sure that there was plenty of wood arranged so that the fire was certain to burn. Neither of us was at all prepared for what happened.

The fire lit very easily. I arranged the kettle over it at the end of a long stick. A gust of wind shot a flame two or three feet long out on to the moss. Little circles of fire began to spread outwards with a crackling sound. Before I had beaten them out another orange streak sent out new circles in a different direction—and before those were neutralized yet more had been created. We beat desperately at the rapidly multiplying points of light, knocked the kettle off and tried to extinguish the blazing wood. But it was well alight and not put out so easily. The moss was now burning several feet away; a dry branch caught fire and flared up angrily. So did another.

"This is too much for us," shouted Arja. "I'll go for help."

Here we were lucky. Perhaps a quarter of a mile back we had passed a small house with—by the mercy of fate—a telephone. Arja raced off to it and I fought the conflagration. I have rarely felt my resources so inadequate. I wasted valuable minutes going for water which was much too far away to be any use; and by that time the fire was roaring through the trees. "Whumph!" —a pile of cut branches ignited with a sound like an explosion, and acrid smoke swirled round me. I could not now even see the limits of the blazing wood and the despairing thought went through me—what can stop this? How can the few people within reach prevent this sweeping uncontrollably through the forest?

It was not as bad as that. I learned, rapidly, that the one way to stop the fire was to tear up the ground in front of it; then I heard a shout through the smoke. Arja reappeared with two or three men equipped with picks and shovels; they dug a trench round the fire, then sat down and waited. The fire roared on consuming the dead wood and blackening the ground till it reached the trench; then it stopped. The noise died and the smoke died away. Once more there was Lapland peace.

It was, in one sense, not a serious fire: no one was injured and no property destroyed. But quite a large area had been burnt; and in the air was the disconcerting thought—what if there had been no help anywhere within reach? We heard, later, that there had been one fire which had needed 300 men to fight it; that, in a district where the total population was around 1,000, must have meant every able-bodied man. It was, in fact, the law that in such an emergency any man in the district could be called on for a certain number of hours without payment.

Though it was now dead, our fire had lasted several hours: and we had by no means finished with it. We were, in fact, under a kind of arrest; we were not allowed to leave the scene of the fire till the local forest supervisor had examined it and questioned us. We waited in no very bright mood. The forest supervisor was some time in coming; I thought we were lucky that it was not raining, then reflected that if it had been the whole affair might never have taken place.

At last he arrived, not very pleased to have to make a long journey to this spot and without any particular admiration for us. In fact, if we had been a couple of tourists, particularly from some other country, we should have been in an awkward situation. We were helped, in fact perhaps saved, by Arja's position. As the Ivalo dentist she treated patients right up to the farther boundary of Utsjoki and for this was regarded as an essential and respected person. When it became clear who she was, the atmosphere altered, and the fire was considered an accident due to inexperience by a useful member of the community; not to be repeated, but yet pardonable. It was still an expensive business; to the damages which were due to the Forest Administration had to be added the cost of the piles of cut wood, which had already been sold; and on top of that was the compensation for loss of time to the fire-fighters. We might have avoided the last-named according to the strict letter of the law but did not choose to do so. The whole cost us over £50.

This should perhaps serve as a warning against lighting fires in Lapland forests. If one needs to do so it is safest to light them on the official camping sites. If you are a wanderer who does not stick to official sites—which is closest to the real Lapland spirit—then you should only light fires on stones near water. If you do have to stop a fire you can do it by digging a trench round, but make the circle of the trench big enough or the fire will be past the trench before it is finished. Having dug the trench, start a counter-fire inwards, so that the advancing flames only meet ashes.

What I was unaware of that day was that my background of experience was wrong. It was a background of England, mixed up with memories of lighting fires in the snow. Snow does not burn, and the state of the ground in England does not change very rapidly. Only six weeks before, in April, we had been lighting fires with perfect safety in the snow on ski-ing trips; it was, to me, very difficult to understand that conditions had so changed in those six weeks that the ground covering was now as inflammable as paper.

The remainder of the day had in it a touch of Gilbertian humour. It was next necessary for us to be questioned by the Utsjoki police authority. Police and legal matters in Utsjoki were the responsibility of one man, Tauno Lakomäki. (He had an assistant at Karigasniemi, but Karigasniemi was an eight-hour journey down the river.) Now, as it happened, we were on our way to stay with a certain Tauno Lakomäki; and it thus followed that our host was responsible for interrogating us.

He came up the river in a boat to meet us. It was a blazingly brilliant day, with great sweeps of sparkling water and glorious stretches of forest coming down to greet them. We chugged along in the open motor boat, and every time we came near a house by the water someone was there, tools nearby, ready to go and fight the fire. Tauno, who was always known as Tane, called out to them to relax, whilst we studied the sky and the water.

We landed at the village of Utsjoki. Ahead of us the Utsjoki River, up which we had been travelling, swept round to meet the Teno River; and on the far side of this rose the Norwegian mountains. We walked along the buff-coloured path past fields of small, bent and contorted trees: dwarf birches. They gave a queer orchard-like impression, as though we were in some new region of space which had orchards, but orchards of a fantastic kind. Utsjoki, then so inaccessible, did feel at that time as though it were only loosely connected with this world.

Utsjoki, the most Lappish commune in Finland, was also the most thinly populated. The Lapps lived in scattered dwellings along the Teno River, or along the post path linking Inari and Utsjoki village. In addition to Utsjoki there was Karigasniemi, a small village in the south-west; and Nuorgam, in the top north-eastern corner. The rest of the Utsjoki commune was filled with hills and forests, with reindeer and fish—and it was these that provided the population with their livelihood.

Utsjoki had no doctor or dentist of its own; these had to come from Ivalo. The nearest chemist was also in Ivalo, a hundred miles away. Utsjoki had, however, its own council, which was sometimes in financial difficulties. The *nimismies* for Inari was responsible for Utsjoki; Tane, our host, was his resident deputy.

The house in which Tane lived stood at one end of the village, with a fence round it and a white gate. It had about as many rooms in it as the average British house; by Lapland standards, therefore, it was big. Tane's wife, Leena, was in the kitchen when we went in; a kettle was boiling on the wood-fired cooker and a big pail of water drawn from the well stood on the table nearby. Leena had been a teacher, and held a master's degree. Tane himself had studied law and might have taken his studies further if the war had not put a stop to them.

After coffee, and food, we went up to our room. The window was standing open as I walked in; and for no reason at all the wind suddenly slammed it to and broke it, scattering the glass on the floor. There was no connection between anything I had done and that window; it was an entirely arbitrary act of nature. Yet I felt guilty; added to the earlier events of the day it seemed to complete the picture of me as an altogether un-desirable guest. We had also still to be examined by Tane.

After some more talk Tane unlocked the door of the police station part at the back and took us in. It was a very gently conducted interrogation, but even in Lapland a police station has a certain atmosphere of formality and I was glad when we came out again.

Then we went on the river.

Or did we? Did we go then or twenty-four hours later? When there is no night, no clear band of darkness between one day and the next, events acquire a certain timelessness. One cannot locate them exactly. Some people in Utsjoki do in fact completely reverse the conventional order in summer, staying up all night and sleeping through the day. But either that day or the next Tane took us along the Teno in his boat.

On the way back, with Finland on the right hand and Norway on the left, we saw four or five fishermen on the Norwegian side. They had just caught a salmon. There is excellent salmon fishing here. Arja became very excited at the sight of the salmon; she had never owned a whole salmon before and decided that she wanted to buy it. The owners were agreeable to this, but there was some discussion as to the price as the salmon had not been weighed. Tane said that he would weigh it, and nobody seemed to have any objections, so we put the salmon into the boat and took it back to Tane's house.

Tane weighed the salmon, cleaned it and cut it up, and at two o'clock in the morning we sat round the table in the sunlight eating fried salmon. The cost of the salmon, 700 marks a kilo, or about 7s. a pound, was less than it would have been in Helsinki and much less than in a hotel; but the difference was not so great as it would have been a few years ago when communications were more difficult.

A day or two after that we returned, with the salmon. Tane took us by boat to the place where the road to Inari began, and set us off along it. Here we ran into trouble again. Kalle, the *nimismies*, had said that he would be coming this way with a party of people who were going to a local court. We believed that his car was going to take us back. Unfortunately there had been a misunderstanding: the car had left before we arrived. There was no alternative transport.

We were left standing forlornly at the end of the road, eighty or ninety miles from home and at least fifty miles from the nearest highway on which buses ever ran. We had no food except a couple of apples, and we had very little money.

We walked three miles down the road; and realized we were very hungry. Suddenly we remembered the salmon. We stopped at one of the old huts, or *autiotupa*, lit a fire—very carefully— in the hearth provided, hacked pieces off the salmon with my *puukko*, the knife which all men carry when travelling in Lapland, and roasted them in the fire at the end of long pieces of wood. We sat for some time over our simple meal, destitute except for fresh salmon.

After a further thoughtful walk we came to a building with telephone wires running to it. We knocked on the door and asked if we could use the instrument, an old-fashioned black cylinder on the wall, and whilst Arja did so I looked around.

This was a Lappish farm. The Lapps have taken to farming in a small way, owning a few animals and a small piece of cleared land with the forest pressing in all round it. No farming is very easy in Lapland, but the visitor can rest assured that any milk he drinks probably comes from a cow. It might be goat's milk, for goats as well as cows are kept in Lapland, but it is unlikely to come from the reindeer.

A farm in south Finland usually has a big, many-roomed house, and its owner, if it is a large one, may be a substantial man. This Lappish farm had one main room. On one side stood the stove, in one corner was a box-bed for some members of the family, and in a second corner a reindeer skin was spread out for the others. From near the reindeer skin an incredibly old man watched us silently. In the middle of the floor was a Singer sewing machine.

Arja finished telephoning; she had been speaking to the taxi station in Ivalo and they had agreed to come and fetch us. A man not quite so old as the incredibly old man asked if we should like some coffee. We told him we liked coffee very much. He nodded understandingly.

"I thought so," he said without moving a muscle of his face. "I've heard about those coffee fires."

The Lapps know a great deal about what goes on, both in Lapland and the world outside. They do not necessarily accept this outer world at quite the valuation it puts on itself, and are capable of making the driest comments on it with perfectly solemn features. Two Lapps taken on a visit to the capital city, Helsinki, to which they had never been, said that they were impressed with what they saw; then added: "But isn't it rather a long way from things?"

The car eventually picked us up some three hours later, when we had tramped further down the hot road. The driver himself looked warm: it had been thirty-five Centigrade (or ninety-five Fahrenheit), he said, that day in Ivalo. This may have been an overestimate, but the summer in Lapland quite often touched thirty Centigrade (or eighty-six Fahrenheit). For a few weeks it was difficult to keep cool.

6 : To the Arctic Ocean

"The way ahead lies with ourselves; we must co-operate across the frontiers."

Erkki Jomppanen,
Internordic Lapp Conference, 1953

THE Teno River is one of the great highways of Finnish Lapland. Together with its tributaries it forms the eastern and northern border of Finland for over 130 miles. Having its origin near the junction of the eastern and western arms of Lapland, it grows steadily in size till finally it sweeps out of Finland, and into Norway, to its destination in the Arctic Ocean. In its earlier stretches it is called the Inari River, or Inarinjoki: but when it crosses the road linking Inari with Norway at Karigasniemi, it becomes the Teno. Before the road from Inari to Utsjoki was finished, the easiest method of reaching Inari from Utsjoki was to come by boat down the Teno till it reached the road, after which normal motor transport could be used.

Like many Lappish rivers, the Teno is not very deep, and there are difficult passages between Karigasniemi and Utsjoki. In winter, however, a way was cleared through the snow on the frozen river, and it was then comparatively easy to drive the whole way by car. Many places in Lapland are, indeed, simpler to reach in winter than in summer.

Towards the end of the summer—that is to say in August —we went to Utsjoki by this other route. We put a large blue rucksack and a small khaki-coloured one into the bus and rode northwards from Inari till we reached the point where the new road to Utsjoki started. Here the bus swung off in the other direction, left towards Karigasniemi on the Norwegian border. There were plenty of passengers at Inari, but they dropped off one by one to isolated farms along the road until at last we were the only two left, riding in a ghostly bus which finally pulled up and stopped for the night.

We climbed out. We were at Tenokoti, a guest house by the Teno itself and on the very edge of Finland. To the left was the main building; to the right, a number of cabins, each just big enough for two, and in one of these we spent the night, with the Teno muttering gently below us.

Tenokoti and its owner, Yrjö von Grönhagen, were both

original. Inside, the building was painted in vivid colours—blue doors framed in orange; seats in yellow and dark red. On the wall was a painting of a Mayor of Lübeck in the seventeenth century, and on each side of it portraits of other gentlemen, with dates from various periods of history. All were signed: Yrjö von Grönhagen. All bore a resemblance to him, but at the end was one with such a striking resemblance that it could —surely—only be a self-portrait. It was, indeed, not only signed but also headed with his name.

Seven languages were spoken at Tenokoti and a variety of nationalities passed through it. One of the other guests—who was neither Finnish nor British—spoke to me in the morning.

"Some people come here for fishing," he said. "I can appreciate that. But some of them don't fish." He waved his hand to the panorama of mountain and river and forest. "They just seem to like to be here." He shook his head sadly. "I can't understand it."

For the true Lapland lover the emphasis is frequently on being—in Lapland—rather than doing.

We left Tenokoti that morning about half past eleven and walked along the river edge for half a mile—a half mile of chalk-white and purple-grey pebbles, sweeping in and out towards the water. We had to reach the post boat by twelve o'clock, when it started on its day-long journey up the river. We found it with a few minutes to spare. It was open, like a large rowing boat, with an outboard motor. In the middle were four seats facing each other, and at one end two more seats and a pile of parcels under a waterproof sheet.

The boat bobbed gently up and down on the water; at one end a man with a cloth cap looked at us. It occurred to me that he was warmly dressed, more than I should have thought necessary on that fine sunny morning. Presently a boy appeared, and stationed himself at the opposite end of the boat to the man. The trio was now complete: postman, postboy and post boat, and all were ready to start.

I had been warned that it would be very cold on the Teno. On the hot summer day when the warning had been given, it had been difficult to believe that anywhere could be cold. Now, looking at the clear cold water, feeling the breeze, and thinking of the eight to twelve hours ahead, I began to wonder if I had paid sufficient attention to that good advice. It was indeed true, as I found later, that travel by boat up the Lapland rivers could be extremely cold—colder than anything else I experienced. It was always a problem on such journeys to realize how warmly clothed one needed to be on the river.

Hastily I started an inverted strip-tease—I tore every pull-over I could find out of my rucksack and put them on one over the other: a modest brown British pullover underneath; a blue and grey Scandinavian one with long sleeves next; over that a thick white Finnish pullover with a roll top sufficient to keep a giraffe's neck warm; and finally, a blue *anorak* tightly laced up. This outfit turned out to be on the light side.

Arja, at the same time, had been re-equipping herself at least as thoroughly and we rolled on board like two plump teddy bears. The boat started off with a noise like an angry hornet. After some time we saw a yellow blob on top of a stick beside the river; as we came nearer it turned into a box with a lid. The noise of the motor subsided into the drowsy bumble of an overfed bee talking in its sleep, the boat slowed down, the postboy rose grasping a bundle of papers, and as we drew level with the yellow box he hurled the bundle towards the bank where it landed on the ground and set pebbles rolling into the river.

The noise of the motor rose again and we were off, dodging from one side of the river to the other until we reached the next post box miles further on. The Teno is not easy to navigate, and at that time was particularly shallow. Once the boat came to a dead stop in the middle of the river, stuck in the sand; Arja and myself, the postboy, and the one other traveller got out and pushed. Later we came to a *köngäs*—a rapidly flowing stretch of water over rocks. This time there was no argument: the passengers were put ashore and told to walk for three miles till they met the boat again.

We journeyed on, a speck on the water between those beautiful, empty hills. At times we passed long stretches of smooth yellow sand; in England any one of them would have been a crowded bathing beach. Here, too far away for any holiday-maker to reach them, they simply existed in idyllic loneliness.

The wind blew chillier and chillier. The boatman had kindly lent us a big cover, and we crouched down under it; but I felt both cold and distinctly hungry. Then—oh joy!— the boat pulled in beside one of those yellow post boxes and stopped. We climbed out and walked up to a Lappish farm, and inside the Lappish farm, laid out ready, were things to eat and hot coffee. It was a real Lappish farm, and the woman there spoke Lappish and not, apparently, Finnish. Indeed, I seemed better able to communicate than Arja. Perhaps that was because she asked for the toilet whilst I asked for the bill.

In this region Lappish is the means of communication

between people on either side of the river. Most speak either Finnish or Norwegian, though not all.

We reached Utsjoki at nine o'clock in the evening. Leena, the wife of Tane, the Utsjoki policeman, came to meet us. Tane was away from home; Leena said he was very tired due to having so many high officials visit him who had to be taken out all night fishing.

We were back on the water at seven o'clock the next morning. In front of us was another four hours' travel up the river to Nuorgam, into the very top corner of Finland. After that we planned to make a wide sweep round through Norway and return to Karigasniemi. I had been warned that the boat on this day would not be so luxurious as the other one. The first boat had seemed to me adequate, though hardly what I should have called luxurious, and I waited with some interest to see what the next one would be like. It differed from the first in being smaller, and having very limited seating accommodation. First-class passengers sat on the part of the floor which was covered by a reindeer skin, the others where they could.

The boat droned off up the river, stopping fairly frequently to pick up passengers, whilst the boatman shouted to his sons in Lappish. It had a peculiar intonation, quite different from Finnish. He sounded to be swearing at the boys, but perhaps he wasn't. What we had not appreciated, however, was that this part of the river also contained a *köngäs*—a fast-moving rocky section past which the boat could not go. It came to this, stopped, and all the passengers got out; we thought at first that we had reached Nuorgam, then found we were seven miles away. We knocked at the first house we saw. The lady of the house said that we might get a lift to Nuorgam if we crossed to the other side of the river.

We managed to find someone with a boat to take us across. There may have been hidden dangers and difficulties in this; if there weren't then I think the charge—1,000 marks or over a pound—was high. Against that must be set the free lift which the owner of a car on the far side generously gave us. We crossed back again and were in Nuorgam. Nuorgam is a tiny village as far as it is possible to get from Helsinki whilst still remaining in Finland: a few houses in a stretch of cleared land by the river, a shop, and Finland's northernmost farm, with a lane running to them. We stayed in a house at one end of the village. It was comfortable enough at that time of the year, but there were sufficient cracks through which the wind penetrated to make me wonder what it would be like in winter. The house was also unusual in being a tiny meteorological station. It had a rain gauge, wet and dry bulb thermometer, and recording barometer. Regular reports were sent out by telephone.

On the other side of the river was a much larger village. This, however, was not in Finland but in Norway. We crossed over the next day; there was no bridge or ferry but it was not difficult to find a local boatman who took us across for a tenth the price we had paid lower down. I fingered my passport anxiously as we landed in Norway; I felt guiltily that I ought to report to somebody. No one gets into England so informally. There was, however, no trace of a Customs' official or even a police station: nobody to report to at all. In the end my wife persuaded me to continue the journey, somewhat uneasily.

It was so easy to cross the border that one might have expected little difference on the other side, a region of transition in which Finnish and Norwegian characteristics were merged. It was not so; one had the feeling that one had walked into quite a different atmosphere. The time was an hour earlier; a purely man-made distinction, but one which could not be ignored. The people we talked to did not seem to understand Finnish. They spoke Norwegian, which of all the Scandinavian languages is perhaps closest to English—so that even without knowing it at all there are words and cadences and intonations which sound familiar. The houses, too, had changed. We spent a long time arguing what made them at once distinguishable from the houses on the Finnish side—whether it was colour, shape, size, or the way they were laid out; but undeniably they were different. We were in Norway.

The Norwegian village was much more accessible than the Finnish one. It was connected by an adequate motor road with the Arctic highway and the coach service which runs through Norway right up to Kirkenes in the extreme north. We had been told that a bus went from the village, but when we made inquiries there seemed to be a good deal of vagueness about this bus. No one knew when it came. No one knew what it looked like. No one had been in it. We sat down by the side of the road without much hope, but to our surprise a perfectly satisfactory bus arrived, apparently laid on specially for us since there was no one else in it except the driver.

It is possible, from this point, to make a broad sweep round Norway either by road or by sea, and re-enter Finland on the western side. We planned to go north-east to Kirkenes, then back by boat. The bus we were on took us only a few miles, to the point where it joined up with the main Arctic highway. There we had an hour or two to wait.

We were hungry; it was only a small place and did not seem to have a superfluity of restaurants or hotels—in fact, it was difficult to find any. At last we found a *gestgiveri*—the Norwegian name for a place to stay, usually simpler and less formal than a hotel. They agreed to give us food in five minutes at one o'clock.

It is always difficult with a restricted knowledge of the language to be quite certain what one has walked into. Not that there was anything sinister about the *gestgiveri*; the dining room, on the contrary, had a clubby, faintly Dickensian atmosphere. We sat at a long table with ten men and ate a good solid Norwegian Sunday dinner. One of them, obviously the chairman, sat next to Arja and made conversation in Norwegian to which she replied in Swedish. The languages are close enough for a reasonable amount of understanding and misunderstanding to occur. The men had come there to fish.

Later the bus took us away from the little village and down the side of the long tongue of sea which came licking inland. We drew away from it, climbing up over high bare country, then dropped down to Kirkenes.

It was raining when we reached Kirkenes, and we hurried damply to the hotel—glowing and attractive against the sobs of rain sweeping down the twilit street—then to the private house to which they sent us since they were full up. Anxious to find this haven as we were, we could not avoid noticing the great Sydvaranger works which dominated the town. There was something strangely familiar about Kirkenes. With its shops and its cinemas, its houses standing neatly in their own gardens, it might have been a cleaned-up version of some Yorkshire industrial town. Lapland had vanished.

Sydvaranger—or its outward aspects—stands on a hill one side of the town, a block of metal and glass buildings terminating in a long angular metal tube which runs down and dips out of sight towards the sea. We were told that you could reach 10,000 people through this firm and that they owned their own school and a local cinema.

We went to a cinema in the evening. It looked terribly dilapidated. Many buildings in Kirkenes had this dilapidated, run-down appearance, and they contrasted strongly with the neat rows of new-looking wooden houses. The cinema had once been painted yellow, and the remains of the paint now clung to it like the last leaves of autumn. The film—a product of the light-hearted Danes—was good, but the wooden seats were hard.

There was another hill on the opposite side of the town. We

walked to the top of it and found a monument. I glanced at it, then stopped with interest and looked more carefully. The monument was dedicated not to Norwegian soldiers, but to Russian. Kirkenes is very close, geographically, to Russia. The writing on the monument said that the Russians mentioned had freed Kirkenes from the German occupation during the war. Kirkenes, therefore, is one of the few Western towns which celebrates its liberation by the Russians. (We were told that such a celebration does take place every year.)

One other foreign influence could be seen in Kirkenes: the conspicuous sign of the consulate of the German Federal Republic.

Close at hand, however, was the sea—and not any sea, but the Arctic Ocean itself. The name, with its suggestion of vast icebergs and extreme cold, was at this season of the year misleading. The water, as next morning we walked up the white metal and wooden gangway on to the deck of the boat, was calm and sunny. At half past eight three men took down the gangway and wheeled it off; just before they did so a woman rushed up and anxiously posted a letter in the letter box at the end. The yellow funnel gave a great belch of black smoke, then the "blunt end" of the ship swung away from the quay-side, ropes were cast off, and the red letters saying "Kirkenes" became smaller and smaller as we sailed towards the hills which locked the harbour.

Scattered silvery clouds drifted over the sky, occasionally casting shadows on the blue-grey of the rocks and the green grass partly covering them. Our destination was Hammerfest: but that was a day and a night away, and before reaching it we had to call at Vadsö, Vardö, and Honningsvåg.

They were attractive little ports. As we sailed towards one of them the sun would suddenly flash from a mosaic of white, green, grey, and yellow—the colourful roofs of the houses. As we neared the harbour the ship's siren gave a great raucous blast which echoed round the hills; then we sailed in gently past the harbour light with its two cylinders of gas, past the three shining needles which were the masts of the wireless station, past the wind indicator distended by the breeze, till we reached the brown quay with its buff harbour building.

The gangway united ship and shore; passengers went up and down it. Seamen in blue jerseys and corduroy trousers swung ropes loosely round grey boxes with metal edges, and over they went to the waiting Douglas truck below. Down there was a medley of horses and carts, bicycles, milk churns, motor cars; barrels with metal bindings; and mysterious boxes covered with tarpaulins. Vegetables went off, and long metal cases loaded with fish came on. Then the book in Arja's hands was trembling again in sympathy with the motion of the engines; above us were white bird bodies tipped with black and yellow beaks spotted with red; the ship was under way again and the gulls were soaring and gliding above it.

A thin golden line of sand marked the division between land and water on the left, with hills rippling back to the faint white glow of the mountains in the distance. On the right, rocks and islands with strange forms rose like primitive creatures from the misty sea.

The atmosphere was becoming less translucent. Suddenly the noise of the engines was muffled, the siren called warn-ingly, and sea, sky, and land all disappeared. We were in a thick white cloud and continued thus for some time.

Arja disappeared into our cabin and I went for a while to meditate in the smoking room. There was little life to be found in it. Four men sat at different tables; sometimes they looked at the Danish newspaper; sometimes they looked at each other; sometimes they just stared into space. The room had one other occupant, a lady, a well-groomed smart-looking Scandinavian who was reading a book near one of the windows. If Adam had been as indifferent to Eve as the men seemed to be to this lady, the human race would never have existed.

Losing interest in the smoking room, I went down and joined Arja in the cabin. Suddenly I noticed a change. The engines had stopped and the boat was almost stationary, sway-ing in the water. We were not due to reach any port: some unknown factor must be delaying us. I went to the upper deck.

The atmosphere was clear. We had left the cloud through which we had been travelling and I could see it some distance behind us. The ship was hardly moving and ahead another cloud was lightly touching the sea. Behind it the sun was shining so that the cloud looked like an enormous grey pillow with pink edges. To the left the land rose sharply out of the water, which was tossing roughly.

In the space between us and the land was a much smaller boat, rolling from side to side in the disturbed sea. It came closer and closer until it was almost alongside, apparently wanting to transfer a passenger to us. A rope jerked towards us, but so violently were the masts moving to and fro that the smaller boat had to draw away again. After a moment or two a third boat, a very small boat, appeared and a young man jumped into it from the second boat; he was then brought alongside and eventually managed to board us. It seemed an adventurous operation to have to undertake whilst carrying a suitcase, as he was.

The engines started again and we disappeared, with the new passenger, into the grey and pink cloud. By the time we reached Hammerfest, however, the clouds had disappeared; from our room in the Grand Hotel we looked out over blue water, with the sun streaming down so brilliantly that the scene looked Mediterranean. Hammerfest is, indeed, a much warmer place than Ivalo; in winter its temperature is nearly twenty degrees higher. That old present from America, the Gulf Stream, is responsible for this; having warmed up England, it wanders on to Scandinavia and makes the coast of Norway much warmer than it looks to be on the map.

In going north from Helsinki one reaches a point—around or south of the junction of Norway and Finland—where cold and wildness are greatest. Further than this, as one approaches the shores of the Arctic Ocean, the temperature increases and one enters a different kind of civilization—the civilization of those who live round the sea.

Next day we took a bus out of Hammerfest along the road which winds around the mountains above the town and the smart white ships in the harbour, across the ferry and on to Skaidi, an isolated road junction in the mountains. At Skaidi we changed into a second bus which took us on to Lakselv, where we spent the night, and the following day a further bus delivered us to Karasjoki, not far from the border of Finland and Norway. The circle was almost completed.

Karasjoki is a village of some size with a school, guest-house, and shops. It is in a very central position in Lapland and when we arrived a conference was taking place—a conference of Lapps from Finland, Norway, and Sweden. There was also a representative from Greenland, though he did not seem to be quite so close a member of the family.

About forty per cent of the delegates wore Lappish costume; the remainder might have been attending any conference anywhere. There was a feeling of incongruity about the conference; of incongruity in seeing this vivid clothing mixed up with bicycles and cars, of hearing the problems of this freedom-seeking life discussed in the staid school hall. In the dining room were two flags: the Union Jack and the Stars and Stripes, a tribute to the presence of one or two English and Americans.

I was also conscious of a strange new allegiance—to our Lapps, to those coming from Finland. Those from Sweden and Norway looked different; the colours had more green amongst

Reindeer round-up : the deer is finally overcome

Reindeer man Heikki, husband of
Ilona, the Sodankylä dentist

Eetu Saarelainen and one of his
daughters at their winter kämppä

Lapps talking together during the sports at Inari

Kolta Lappish
woman with
characteristic
head-dress

them than I was accustomed to. And was it true that the prosperity of Sweden showed even here—that the Swedish Lapps were more lavishly dressed?

The languages used were Finnish, Norwegian, Swedish and Lappish. Each speech was translated into two other languages, so the proceedings moved slowly. But there is no doubt of the importance of this conference and those that have preceded and followed it. They express the natural unity of Lapland; and they provide one of the few opportunities which the Lapps have for expressing their needs with some degree of effectiveness.

It was different from any other conference at which I have been present because it was concerned with the whole way of life of a people—and behind it always was the thought: can this continue? It ranged widely over Lapp living conditions, history, and language: but most prominent were the two key subjects of the right to use natural resources and education. For the Lapps who lived by reindeer herding and fishing, the protection of these from interference was of the utmost importance. Also of great concern to them was the question of how children should be educated so as to fit them for that kind of life, or alternatively to allow them to make their way in competition with non-Lapps.

Of the odd pictures that stuck in my memory, one is of an old Lapp man, obviously not rich, sitting at one end of a bench on which were three non-Lapps. Someone spoke to him in Swedish; he shook his head and said, *"Puhun Suomi"* ("I speak Finnish"). He rose to go, leaning heavily on his two sticks; not the neat manufactured English kind, but simple rough branches with knobs at the end. He wore the blue costume edged with red and orange of the Finnish Lapps and round his legs were the soft wrappings of dark brownish-red Lappish boots. He smoked a little short stick of a pipe with a whitish bowl at the end. His face expressed neither hope nor despair, but acceptance; acceptance that life was hard, but belief that it had got to be lived. He went away, back to his isolated, primitive life, and his own Lappish thoughts.

The next time we had news of him, he said: "I haven't heard anything about this chap Nasser for two days. What's he doing now?"

We got a lift over the border in a car. I was going home, yes, to my family, to where I was living, to where there were friends —and yet I was going away from any familiar language sounds, away from that feeling that only nineteen hours by sea separated me from England. We were going home, yet—so it seemed

—a thousand miles further from London. I could never cross that border without feeling a peculiar jerk inside myself.

We arrived home in the evening; Ivalo is about three hours by road from the border. A traveller has one sadness in his soul: he sees a little bit from many stories and the end of none. What happened to the little Lapp boy we saw on the way back from Hammerfest? He ran across the road in front of the bus with a dog and another little white creature that might have been a lamb; and after we had passed he rushed back into the road again. Did the bus hit the lamb or merely frighten it? The vehicle rushed on, as impatient and inexorable as the civilization that produced it; and watching that civilization pushing itself over Lapland one wanted to cry the old Latin saying: *festina lente*—hasten slowly!

7 : Dentist and Doctor in Lapland

THE Ivalo dentist is in one particular set of circumstances extremely unfortunate. What does she do when her own tooth aches? There is no other dentist nearer than Rovaniemi, or at the best Sodankylä, a hundred miles away, and the Ivalo dentist is far too busy to travel this distance. The day one of Arja's teeth began to hurt we decided quickly that the only possible solution was to ask the doctor to extract it for her.

Doctors are theoretically capable of doing this part of a dentist's work, though some of them are extremely reluctant to take it on. One young substitute doctor, confronted with a similar problem, walked up and down saying in a loud voice to the nurse:

"This is going to be interesting. I've never taken a tooth out before. I wonder what it will be like. I shall learn a lot from this . . . by the way, where is the patient?" But the horrified patient had disappeared.

Esko Taulaniemi, the commune doctor when we first arrived in Ivalo, was, however, quite different from this. Tall, and with a long thin face, he intended to practise surgery and hence carried out operations in the Ivalo hospital. These would otherwise have had to go to Rovaniemi, five or six hours away by road. He went about with a sleek black dog with a touch of wolf in it, and drove, hard, a black Armstrong Siddely saloon. He had just come through a bad skid; his car met two reindeer at seventy m.p.h. on the snow-covered Rovaniemi road and overturned.

We went to see Esko. Esko's wife, who spoke English, had been a nurse; I talked to her whilst Esko and Arja disappeared into Esko's surgery. They returned some time later with Arja lacking a tooth, which, she told me feelingly, had had three roots.

The professions usually have a high standing in a Finnish country commune. A great deal of use is made of professional titles; Arja (like dentists generally) was addressed as "doctor". It took me some time to realize that sentences beginning, "Would the Doctor and the Engineer . . ." meant Arja and myself.

The work, however, was killing. There had been no dentist in the commune for nearly two years and the teeth of the school

67

children were in a bad state. Lappish children have as great a
fondness for sweets as other children but exist on a more
monotonous diet. Fruit is expensive, and green vegetables not
eaten with great enthusiasm. We found it difficult to persuade
our helpers to serve green stuff, although they were specifically
told to buy these things. They seemed to regard such greenery
as unsuitable for human beings.

From morning till late in the evening the whirring of the
drill was rising and falling in the surgery.

The commune doctor has even greater standing than the
dentist; and still more killing work. Esko was the only doctor
for the commune of Inari and also for the still more northerly
one of Utsjoki. He was responsible for nearly 8,000 people. On
finding this out I rather tactlessly asked:

"How many undertakers are there in this commune?"

The doctor has one consolation. People do not come to him
very often with trivial complaints. If you have to travel all day
by boat or reindeer to get there you don't go to tell the doctor
you have a slight cold. In a real emergency the doctor had to
reach the patient or the patient come to the doctor by plane;
this happened perhaps twice whilst we were in Inari commune.

Country communes sometimes go to great lengths to get a
doctor: in one rural district in Finland the council built a
house costing £9,000 for the doctor and was then unable to
persuade one to come.

There is a tendency for the medical profession to mate
within itself, for doctors to marry nurses and for dentists to
marry dentists. I, therefore, felt as though I had suddenly been
pulled inside a new world from which in the past I had tried to
keep away. We belonged, Arja by right and I as her spouse by
courtesy, to the group of people who cared for the welfare of
the human body. Closely connected with both doctor and
dentist was the chemist, or *apteekkari*, Henni Hietala, who
lived in a new wooden house on the main street with a little
girl she had adopted.

In Finland the training of anyone who owns a dispensary is
exceptionally thorough. It is first necessary to qualify as a pharmacist, a training about as long as that in England; but the
qualified pharmacist is only allowed to work under the direction of a more experienced person known as a *provisoori*. To
become a *provisoori* it is necessary to work for some years as a
pharmacist, and then study for·four or five years more. The
provisoori is still not allowed to open an independent business,
but must have further experience. Finally, a new pharmacy can
only be started in an approved place; where an opening occurs

there are usually several applications from which one is chosen by the Finnish Medical Council. The chemist cannot, therefore, be a very young person, but has an undoubted standing in the community. Some people go so far as to say "an old *provisoori* knows more than a young doctor". The training of the *provisoori* is longer and in a small place the relationship with the customers is peculiarly intimate. For years they have been bringing prescriptions from the doctor to the chemist, and talking about their various troubles—so that the *provisoori* knows pretty well what to give them.

The prestige of the *apteekkari* is further enhanced by the sharp division that is made in Finland between a *kemikalia*, which sells razor blades, soap, toilet preparations and so on, and an *apteekki*, which deals only with the preparation of medicines and drugs. The *apteekki* is usually a sober, almost religious building with long rows of marked bottles on polished wooden shelves.

There is, in Finland, no free health service, though help is given through the department of social welfare to those who need it. The commune doctor and dentist are supposed, however, to examine each school child once a year. Our commune was in one respect unusual. The children are normally given a preliminary examination at the school, then go for treatment to the place where the doctor or dentist works. In Inari commune this was impossible: it was the biggest commune in Finland, with twelve schools most of which were a very long way from Ivalo. If the children had been required to come to Ivalo it might, in some cases, have meant taking a week off to have a tooth out.

Some, at any rate, of the children would have probably regarded this as a good thing, but in the opinion of the school authorities it was not suitable, and so the dentist (and doctor) had to visit the schools and carry out treatment there. This sometimes involved days and nights away from home, travel where the roads were primitive or even where there were no roads at all. For this purpose we had a complete set of portable equipment: a collapsible chair and a foot-operated drill. The latter was later exchanged for an electric one since most of the schools—cut off from civilization though they were—had their own small generating set.

A dental party consisted of:

1 Collapsible dental chair, in grey carrying case;
2 Movable drill, in pieces, together with lamp;
3 Set of small tools, for operating on teeth;

4 Portable sterilizer;
5 Alcohol (for cleaning only);
6 My wife;
7 Miss Junttila.

At first it gave me cold shivers to think that a dental surgery was part of our home. I would look in, if I needed to speak to Arja, call out my message and hastily withdraw before I saw some horrible sight. It seemed to me a shocking thing then that anyone should disturb the dentist in the middle of what was— so Arja's dental textbooks said—a delicate surgical operation.

Later I hardened up and began to take part in some of the ancillary activities. The commune, though not rich, had furnished the surgery with completely new instruments. They had a very international air: the chair was English; the electric drill French; the sterilizer German; and an auxiliary drill bought later came from Denmark. One difficulty in dealing with such instruments in Ivalo was that usually no one nearer than Helsinki knew much about them: and the makers believed that everyone understood the same language that they did. One had to be a linguist, or just guess.

The equipment included an X-ray set. This was very useful, since some of the Lappish patients had come great distances; they were prepared to wait in Ivalo patiently, but it was difficult to ask them to come again. An X-ray could often show the cause of trouble, but the results needed to be available quickly, so I started developing the X-rays on the premises. Developing a dental X-ray, though it sounds impressive, is a simple operation. It was made more ticklish here since it had to be done in the bathroom, which was also a toilet, laundry, and water supply for the surgery. Later, when more room was available, this service was refined until we could boast that ten minutes after sitting in the chair we could tell you what had to be done.

I also went out to the schools sometimes and helped in the preliminary examinations. Dentists have a way of counting teeth from the centre of the mouth, plus for the top and minus for the bottom; the teeth needing attention were marked on cards which I filled up whilst Arja called out the details. Bending over some boy or girl she would say what sounded like a mathematical formula:

"All sevens missing, all sixes carious, four plus filling, baby minus five to be extracted *nyt saat mennä.*" The last words told the child that he or she could go and the little victim skipped off happily out of the classroom.

It was depressing to see the state of their teeth; in one school of sixty-six children only one had a mouth free from dental decay and which had not needed previous repairs. At first I found it difficult to mark off the cards as quickly as Arja could carry out the examinations; later I became deeply interested in each case, since the whole dental history of the child could be seen in a flash, and I would raise queries: "Have you forgotten about minus six? That was marked as needing a filling last year. Has it been done?"

I nearly lost my job with the dentist twice: in the beginning for being too slow, and at the end for arguing too much.

There were various incidents and misunderstandings from time to time in the surgery. Some of the Lapps showed great calmness and placidity both in the waiting room and in the chair. They were prepared to sit there for long periods without impatience, and didn't complain about the treatment.

This calmness was once unfortunate. Arja had injected an anaesthetic into one side of a Lapp's mouth and was then called away. On returning she extracted a tooth; the Lapp had a bad mouth. Then, as he was leaving, a horrible doubt suddenly struck her. "Yes," he said in answer to her question, "I thought it was funny that you put the injection in one side and then took out a tooth from the other; but I didn't like to mention it."

I, too, occasionally caused surprise to a patient. There were times when I found myself alone in the house apart from Lilian; and the telephone rang. I was seriously tempted to let it ring rather than struggle to answer it in Finnish; but there was always the fear that the call might be from a bleeder, that is to say a person whose tooth had gone on bleeding and refused to stop. Fortunately these were very rare indeed. So I always tried, at least tried, to explain the situation either over the telephone or to personal callers.

"The dentist is away for a little while," I said to one inquirer. "Come back in an hour." He went away with a peculiar look on his face: a Lapland look of acceptance, but with undoubted surprise underneath. I could not understand it and when Arja returned I repeated very carefully my exact words.

"Oh dear," she said, "you told him to come back in a year!"

Dwellers in remote areas naturally tried to make the most of each visit to the centre of things; it was by no means uncommon for a man to come to Ivalo, bring his older children to school, himself come to have his teeth attended to, and take his wife to see the doctor. Others came only once in their lives, when they had all their teeth removed and a complete artificial denture made.

The making of these dentures fascinated me. Once the impression had been taken, the actual fabrication of the denture had to be done by a dental technician, and there was no technician nearer than Rovaniemi, 180 miles away. So, Miss Junttila wrapped the impression in tissue paper, packed it in a cardboard box, tied it with one knot, and took it to the post bus. It travelled for eight hours over a Lapland road, then a day or two later came back similarly. It had to make this trip three times; yet there were hardly ever any breakages.

Doctor, dentist, and chemist may all at one time or another find themselves under pressure to satisfy requirements which are not strictly medical. Alcohol is in Finland a state monopoly, and the establishments where spirits can be bought are strictly limited, especially in the country; and at the time we were in Lapland alcohol could not be sent by post. The nearest place to Ivalo at which one could buy alcohol for home consumption was Rovaniemi. The only places where anyone could go for an alcoholic drink were the hotel at Ivalo and the one at Inari. Apart from that, thirsty persons had to go either to Rovaniemi or to Norway. The management of the hotels therefore had considerable control over any disorderliness; they could simply threaten the offender with exclusion, a threat usually quite sufficient.

The official consumption of alcohol per head in Finland is not high. There is also, however, the unofficial consumption—from private stills and from drinks made from alcohol obtained from other than recognized channels. Scent, which can have an alcoholic content as high as eighty per cent, is used by some. The doctor can, if he thinks it necessary, prescribe alcohol freely; and the dentist has the power to order a certain quantity each month *pro auctore*—for her own use. It therefore happens that men sometimes approach the dentist with discreetly lowered voices, asking if "the doctor" would—perhaps —have a little alcohol to spare. They may also suggest to the commune physician that a certain amount of alcohol is absolutely necessary to their health.

Real drinkers in Finland usually drink only high alcoholic content beverages.

Women in Finland have a long tradition of independence, and have taken a bigger hold of some professions than in England. This is particularly true of dentistry; most Finnish dentists are women, some of them very attractive. In Ivalo during one period women entirely ran the medical services. The health centres—of which there were three in the commune, at Ivalo, Inari, and Sevetti, which were really the first

line of defence, particularly in those regions remote from the
doctor—were all staffed by women; dentist and chemist were
women; and after Esko Taulaniemi left, the new doctor, Mirja
Lehmus, was a woman. The heads of the three schools in
Ivalo were women; and it was strange to find that when so
much could be trusted to them—the entire process of birth,
education, sickness, and dying—hardly a woman appeared on
the governing body of the commune, the *Kunnanvaltuusto*,
or local council. There was, in fact, one amongst twenty
men.

Children were occasionally frightened in the surgery and
refused to have treatment; but others were quite tough. Arja
asked one small girl if it hurt.

"It does that," the girl replied, "but go ahead!"

Some children, indeed, had a positive liking for the surgery.
The chemist's small niece, aged three, would persuade her
aunt to bring her within our precincts and then insinuate herself into the surgery. She would climb on to the chair, glare at
Arja and say in a hoarse whisper: "Drill!" As the drill started
its ominous whirring her eyes would light up with sinister glee.

Because of the limited number of rooms Lilian had frequently slept in the surgery; after the last patient had gone,
the windows of the room had been flung open for a few
minutes, then closed, and the baby wheeled in and placed just
behind the dental chair, where she slumbered very peacefully.

We began to have feelings, however, that some change was
necessary. One evening we went to see Kalle, the *nimismies*,
and his wife Sirkka. The Ivalo River made a broad sweep
round before it ran under the bridge in the centre of Ivalo;
and tucked into this bend was a residential area in which the
houses nestled cosily among the trees, separated, but not too
far separated, from each other. Kalle's house—the official residence of the sheriff—was situated here. It had a white fence
round it, which was unusual in Ivalo, where the boundaries of
houses were often indicated in a very sketchy way; in winter
particularly, ski-ers usually took the most direct route irres-
pective of whose land it went over.

It was a pleasant house; we drank coffee in a room filled with
pictures and heads of animals that Kalle had shot, with the
river running peacefully by not very far away. On the
way home Arja was very thoughtful; suddenly she said to
me:

"There's a house going to be empty on the other side of the
bridge. It doesn't often happen here where there isn't much
room to spare. Shall we go and look at it?"

We went; and eventually we took the house, becoming the tenants of a man called Eränen. It put our expenses up, since it cost 40,000 marks a month (about forty-five pounds), whereas the flat had only cost 30,000, which had been paid by the commune as part of the inducement offered to a dentist to come. It was, in fact, one of the biggest houses in the district, but constructed on the principle of plenty of space per room rather than many rooms. When we went in it had two rooms up above and three—plus a big kitchen—down below. Sliding doors allowed two of these rooms to be combined to give an open space fifteen yards long, which was big enough for parties and meetings. At the front was an enclosed veranda, an excellent place from which to watch the midnight sun in summer and the aurora in winter.

The heating of the house also had to be paid for—all through the Lappish winter. This cost much less than might have been expected. The house itself was very well built: between the outer wooden wall and the inner were several layers of insulation, paper, foil, and sawdust. The double windows were sealed up at the beginning of winter, apart from one or two opened each day for a short time; and down in the cellar was a boiler capable of taking pieces of wood nearly a yard long, with space for storing enough wood to last a couple of months or more. It was hardly necessary to heat the house at all until the outside temperature fell below freezing point, and the total cost for the year came to about 70,000 marks (seventy-seven pounds). That kept the whole house warm enough for us to walk about it in dressing gowns, if we wanted, and (I estimate) would be less than it would have cost to produce the same effect throughout the British winter in the tiny house in Haslemere.

I managed to persuade the boiler to keep going all through the night, eight or nine hours on one loading; some of our friends were not so fortunate with their houses and boilers and had to get up in the small hours of the morning in order to go down to the cellar to re-start the heating. The chemist was particularly unfortunate and had to operate a shift system in which someone rose every two hours during the night.

Eränen, our landlord, was a tall, bulky man with gold-rimmed glasses who lived in Rovaniemi. He spent a good deal of time putting the house in order and did everything we asked. He appreciated my efforts to converse in Finnish and once startled me by saying:

"The engineer speaks Finnish like a horse."

"Really?" I stammered out, not knowing which way to

take it. No horse I have yet met has spoken Finnish. Inquiries made later, however, revealed that this was a compliment, a Finnish idiom meaning that one spoke fluently.

We set up the surgery in one of the upper rooms, with a fine view along the river and across the hills. Most of the equipment reached there safely; a major casualty was the dental chair, which arrived jammed in its highest position and would not come down. For some time Arja had to stand on a stool to deal with tall patients. This lasted until one day Jaakko, the commune secretary, came for treatment. He was a heavy man, and as soon as he sat in it the chair collapsed.

Lilian rapidly settled down in the new house; indeed she regarded almost too much of it as her territory.

"Let the young child follow mother around and watch her at work," said one of the books on how to bring up children. Lilian began putting this into practice. She would crawl up the stairs muttering to herself *"Hampaita! Hampaita!"* ("Teeth! Teeth!"). If rejected at the door of the surgery she would cry bitterly, and watch for the first moment when she could slip in. Her powers developed rapidly, and she began to study the box on the floor which controlled the speed of the drill. "Lilian, leave that pedal alone!" I would hear the dentist cry as the instrument suddenly speeded up with an ecstatic whoop.

As soon as the last patient had gone Lilian would rush into the surgery and climb into the chair; she would point with a tiny finger to the back of her mouth and spit vigorously into the spittoon. She loved the polisher and would laugh gleefully when given a touch of the drill. In the evening she would seize on any nearby person, sit them on the floor and insist on examining their teeth, frequently with the most unsuitable tools.

I myself came to take the surgery more and more for granted, and soon had no inhibitions about walking in and out of it quite freely. It became increasingly difficult to work downstairs at all, since Lilian regarded all this as her territory and noisily and incessantly demanded admittance to any room from which she was excluded, with pathos in her voice. Eventually we decided to make a sanctuary of the surgery, and exclude Lilian from it firmly during working hours. I moved a desk in. It was a fair-sized room with ample space for me as well as the various dental activities. I found the atmosphere rather good for writing: there was a feeling of quiet and concentration, yet with sufficient distraction to be slightly stimulating. There was, also, always the chance that a really colourful figure might come in—a man in full Lappish clothing or a woman with a Kolta Lapp head-dress.

Our establishment was unlike any British household in which I had lived. One does not usually lock doors during the day in Lapland; and in any case it was necessary to allow free access to the waiting room on the upper floor. In the early days Eränen frequently came over to supervise alterations and repairs, and quite often either a plumber or an electrician was on the job. The girls who worked for us had their own life and friends, and Lilian had by this time acquired a number of acquaintances whom she treated with an air of royal command. People also came to see me in connection with English lessons, and dwellers in distant parts who arrived and could not find the surgery tried opening every door until they did.

One unfortunate boy once arrived at the back door too shy to explain what he wanted. He was shot up to the surgery for dental treatment, which he hastily refused; asked if he wanted to learn English, which he didn't; offered to the maid as a possible acquaintance and rejected as too young; offered to Lilian on similar terms and turned down as too old.

Fortunately his shyness finally relaxed just sufficiently for him to explain that he wanted to meet a man who was working in the cellar.

8 : Sevetti and the Kolta Lapps

THERE was a comfortable and homely atmosphere about Fetsi, our home helper, as she sat with the big baking bowl on her knees and her dark head bending over it, or drew from the oven a dish of fresh *pulla*—the sweetened bread which we used to eat with coffee. She seemed very much at home in our establishment—whether dealing with the oven, the baby, or the radio set. With the last-named she was particularly expert; if I did not quickly tune in the required programme Fetsi would at once take over, expertly adjusting the set with a touch of contempt for the inexperienced such as myself.

Yet Fetsi came from the most isolated group of Lapps in Finland, who lived in one of its most inaccessible places—Sevetti. She was a Kolta (or Skolt) Lapp, and was just old enough to have been born in the original home of the Kolta Lapps. This was on the extreme eastern edge of Finland, as it was before the war, and in territory which is now governed by Russia. It could be reached only by long paths through the forest, or by river. Before Finland became independent in 1918 the Kolta Lapps had their own council and to a considerable extent governed themselves. They lived by fishing and reindeer keeping. They had the reputation of being first-rate reindeer men. We once asked Fetsi how old she was when she first drove her own reindeer. "Oh, about seven," she replied, and changed the subject. She didn't seem very keen to talk about her—to me—very fascinating background.

Reindeer usually move from certain definite areas in winter to others in summer, and certain regions may be recognized as belonging to a particular man or family. Semi-permanent dwellings can thus be set up in these places. The Kolta Lappish reindeer made four moves. They went to the spring position until the young reindeer were born, some time in May; next to the summer pasturing grounds; away again in autumn; and finally to the winter home.

Of these the winter home, or winter village, was the most firmly established. One can live with little protection in the short Lappish summer; a light tent is sufficient; but in the cold season one looks for something more substantial. The winter village, therefore, consisted of a row of small wooden houses. In 1938 this little community in Suonikylä—as the place was called—was still only a little influenced by contact with the outside world. It was at that time surveyed by Karl Nickul, the geologist, who proposed that the way in which such a society changed under the influence of the outer world should be studied by repeating the survey at intervals of a few years. There would be then some chance of preventing change being too rapid and of preserving the best values of the old life.

All this was shattered to pieces by the war. When the first planes flew overhead some of the Kolta Lapps stared up in amazement, never having seen anything like that before. Some had not seen a car or even a road. When she was very young, too young to remember clearly, Fetsi was taken away with the other Kolta Lapps, refugees from the struggle moving over the eastern boundary of Finland.

The Kolta Lapps were under some disadvantages compared with the other Lapps. They were regarded as the most primitive Lappish group and housed in meeting halls instead of farmhouses like the others. They were also, perhaps, thought to be under Russian influence. This was quite untrue politically; but culturally they had drawn a good deal from the east. They belonged, not to the Lutheran Church which dominates Finland, but to the Orthodox Church which was the old Church of Russia. According to tradition, their independence and lands had been guaranteed to them by Peter the Great of Russia. Fetsi was a member of this Church, and went once a week to teach children in the little building where Orthodox services were held in Ivalo.

Kolta Lappish, which is a separate and distinct variety of Lappish, also has in it many words taken from Russian. In our household this caused some curious familiarities, since Russian —despite its forbidding appearance—does belong to the same language group as English, whilst Finnish does not. Once hearing me say the word "bottle" Fetsi's face lit up. "Why, that's a Kolta Lappish word," she said. Many of the Kolta Lapps had also adopted Russian surnames: Fetsi's family name was Feodoroff, and another girl who worked for us for a short period was called Semenoff. Fetsi was too young to remember much of the old ways. After the war her education had been completed at the continuation school in Ivalo, through which all children in the commune who did not go to a secondary school had to pass. It was modern, well equipped, centrally heated, lit by electricity and had up-to-date sanitation. She was, therefore, familiar with the conveniences of modern civilization; and she liked them.

"Is life better here or in Sevetti?" I asked her once. She turned and gave me a significant look.

"Here," she said, and there was no doubt in her voice.

She was on the way out from the old life; and, watching her, one realized with a shock that in one generation it was possible to go from one of the most ancient ways of life of Europe almost into our modern ways of thinking and acting. Almost, but not quite. Occasionally a trace of a different culture showed through. During the first Christmas in Lapland we brought out the Christmas Angels, the three little golden figures that went round and round gently striking their two bells as the heat from four candles rose underneath. Suddenly I glanced at Fetsi's face: she was staring at the figures with a child-like expression of wonder. Just a look; yet thinking of it one realizes that it is just this expression we have trained ourselves not to have. We look at things as though we understood them, or expected to very shortly; we give them explanations in terms of the framework of ideas in which we have been brought up; but we very rarely permit ourselves this look of direct acceptance and amazement that things should be so.

The radio set also came to understand that people with varying backgrounds were living in the house. If Arja had been listening it was left tuned to a Finnish programme; if I had been listening, to a station which had recently sent out an English programme; and if Fetsi had been listening, to the last station which had sent out a Lappish programme.

Lapps are supposed to possess special powers of communicating with each other. It is very easy to accept or reject beliefs like this and much harder to find verifiable facts; and powers like this, if they exist, might also show themselves in a less obvious way as a heightening of normal sympathy. Fetsi did seem to possess an exceptional ability to sense what was wanted, even though at the beginning she spoke no English and I spoke hardly any Finnish. One morning I woke up with an uneasy stomach. I went into the kitchen. "I don't want any coffee this morning," I said to my wife in English. "Would you put some hot water on?"

Fetsi (who, remember, at this time knew no English), immediately turned round and said in Finnish: "There's some here already."

There are many tales concerning these supposed telepathic powers of the Lapps.

"Why do you sit in front of a tree when you wish to communicate with someone?" asked a visitor, referring to one supposition.

"Because we haven't got the telephone in our village yet," replied the Lapp addressed, crossly.

We visited the home of the Kolta Lapps that summer and autumn. This was in a quite different place from their original home in Suonikylä; the new boundary drawn after the war put all this in Russian territory. At that time the Kolta Lapps seemed in a parlous condition. They were a small group of only some 400 people, with a way of life remote from the modern world; their lands had gone; what could be done for them? In view of the difficulties it seems remarkable that anything was done, that the former life could at all be set in motion again. It is interesting that some help came at this time from England. A broadcast appeal was made by Flora Robson, the actress; it was initiated by Robert Crottet, a writer particularly interested in the Kolta Lapps.

The Kolta Lapps were finally settled around the lake of Sevetti. This is perhaps as far away from roads and towns as it is possible to get in Finland—and Finland is not thickly populated. A simple, standard house was built for each family; but these were placed in a different way from those in the old winter village. The houses were a considerable distance apart. At one point a health centre and school were built. The school is the most inaccessible in Finland.

Arja went first to Sevetti, carrying out her duty—as commune dentist—to see the school children throughout the commune. The effect of this trip into the wilderness was heightened since at the same time I was discussing my thesis with the examiners in London. I had been working as hard as I could on this since I had arrived in Ivalo and had just managed to slip it in before the end of the University year. It dealt with a rather abstract piece of electronic theory; during those few months in Lapland it had come to seem increasingly unreal. It was difficult, in Lapland, to believe that such problems had any meaning.

I was three weeks in London. Going was a sharp psychological shock; and so was returning. In Ivalo the rest of the world had come to seem remote. The Lapland morning paper arrived in the evening; the Helsinki paper came two days late; and the British Sunday papers usually got there by the following Friday. The outside world, like the stars, existed but was too distant to affect us. In London that tiny little spot in empty space—marked Ivalo—seemed as distant as the moon.

During this time I was entirely out of contact with Arja. She had gone on her journey to Sevetti, up the long Inari Lake and then over the chains of lake and necks of land which stretch out

(Above) Dead tree by Lake Inari; *(below)* tractor in the water un-
loading cable, Lake Inari

Setting off from Menesjärvi

The walk to Lemmenjoki

from its north-eastern corner until finally she reached the Sevetti school and health centre. It was no use writing, since the post motor boat only goes once a week up Inari, and the letters have a further long journey after that.

It was not till much later that I extracted the details of the trip from Arja. They started from Ivalo one fine morning in June—Arja, the Sevetti health sister who had been visiting Ivalo, the Ivalo Commune Master Builder and two other men; also the dental equipment. They travelled in an open motor boat—not very much more than a big row-boat—up the lake until in the evening they reached Partakko, at the end of the lake, where there is a school. Here they stopped overnight. In the morning they started off overland, and about noon arrived at the next lake—a far smaller one than Inari.

"Here," said Arja, "there should have been a man to meet us at twelve o'clock, with a boat. He wasn't there."

"So what did you do?"

"Waited. What else could we do? No hurry in Lapland—he came at three."

They went on for twenty kilometres or so up this lake—Nitsijärvi—stopping for coffee in what Arja described as "a shocking-looking hut on an island", and again at the end of Nitsijärvi in a Kolta Lappish house.

"There were three types of standard house," Arja explained. "This was the biggest. It had one room and a kitchen."

After that they walked again to the next lake.

"But how about all the dental things?" I asked. "How did you get them there?"

"We had porters—you know, like Africa. Some men came to meet us each time we had to go from one lake to another. We all carried something, though." She smiled a rueful smile. "I don't remember what I carried—but there was plenty for each."

Arja thought for a minute, then went on. "Then the Kolta Lapps came. They had heard the dentist was coming, and as we were only thirty kilometres from the health centre they thought that was quite near enough to join the party. They brought their children, *komses* and all."

The *komse* is a wooden cradle, shaped like a small boat. The child is bound into this; the *komse* and the child can then be either hung up to rock gently or carried round with the parents on their wanderings.

"How many lakes did you go over altogether?" I wanted to know.

"Four. As we got near to Sevetti the Kolta Lapps dropped

off to stay with their friends. We did the last bit in a rowing boat and arrived about three or four o'clock in the morning. It was quite light, of course."

During that month it was light all night in Lapland, so there was no problem of darkness. They had, however, suffered from the "ladies with the violins"—the mosquitoes, which are worst in July.

They stayed a few days in Sevetti, then returned by the same route. There was no electricity, and dental examinations had to be made with a flash lamp.

"On the way back," Arja recounted, "I set up what must have been the most primitive dental surgery in Europe. So many people were complaining about their teeth at one point that I stopped in one of the houses and dealt with them. The main room of the house was the surgery and the kitchen was the waiting room. The patients sat on an ordinary chair with a bucket on one side, and the dentist was dressed in trousers, rubber boots, and a sporty blouse."

My own trip to Sevetti was made under conditions that were, by comparison, highly civilized. By that time a small seaplane was available, based on Inari; and one autumn day we went in this. It was quite a large party, with doctor, dentist, two nurses, and Miss Junttila, Arja's dental nurse; a considerable proportion of the medical resources of the commune. It gave me a cold feeling when travelling with the doctor sometimes to think how unpleasant our position would be if we had an accident in which he were involved. One becomes careful of the life of the doctor when he is the only one for over a hundred miles.

It was a pleasant day in September when we set out in one of the Ivalo taxis. In autumn, in Lapland, there is a sudden and unbelievably brilliant flash of colour—the swan song of the departing summer. The sharply falling temperatures combined with the very dry atmosphere give the dying leaves a vividness of colour all the more remarkable because it is so short lived. This is the time of *ruska*, at the beginning of September, when the birches stand like tongues of yellow flame and the ground is a voluptuous mosaic of red ripening berries, dark oval green leaves with the brown mushrooms pushing through, and underneath the light green reindeer moss. The atmosphere is clear and keen and there is still light well into the evening. The magnificent sunsets paint the sky as alluringly as the earth, but with a different technique: the interweaving of a myriad separate strands is replaced by great masses of glowing colour flung on with careless genius.

The lake looked very blue when we reached Inari and the white and red houses stood out against the golden brown of the trees. By the side of the landing stage a small seaplane was moving gently to and fro. It looked much, much smaller than the planes which flew between Helsinki and London, or even up to Ivalo. It could, actually, take seven passengers. We straggled across the landing stage towards it.

Two young men came hurrying round the edge of the lake, apparently the pilot and his assistant. They climbed into the plane and started to fiddle with it.

There was a long delay.

Suddenly the propeller made a convulsive movement, and from inside the engine came a flash and a bang. One of the young men climbed out.

"We shan't be going today," he said briefly.

My private reaction to this was "Thank God"; I thought the plane could do with a careful examination and possibly some new parts. The rest of the party, however, were highly indignant; they pointed out to the pilot that not only had their extremely valuable time been wasted, but also that they had been involved in the expense of a taxi from Ivalo to Inari, for which they expected to be reimbursed. He firmly denied any responsibility; for one dreadful moment I thought he might offer to tie the plane together and take us; then the party broke up with a feeling that it had been ill-used, and we went back to Ivalo.

Two or three days later we tried again. This time our spirits were damped by an old man with whiskers. He walked on to the landing stage as we were climbing into the plane; looked at it thoughtfully, then said, "You ought to pray to God before getting into that thing!"

We got into the air, however, without any trouble. The *ruska* season was at its far end; the colours had lost their early sharpness, yet still possessed a mellow loveliness; and we flew steadily over a purple-and-copper landscape. Below, yellow-brown and reddish trees extended in uncounted number to the horizon, broken up here and there by the duller colours of the marsh; to the right and ahead the blue lake swelled out, broader and broader. Its waters were broken by thousands of islands, ranging from tiny rocks to great expanses on which one could almost get lost. Often one saw the land narrow to a thin isthmus between two lakes, with glowing golden sand on each side; and occasionally—but very, very rarely—a house. Then we circled over the school and church of Sevetti and came sweeping across the lake towards a crowd of children who had rushed out to meet us.

The plane stopped, and we waded ashore. A pair of good rubber boots are a first necessity when travelling in Lapland. Whilst the rest of the party went into the school to inspect the children, I walked round. There was the school, a wooden building with a fence round; the *asuntola* in which the children lived; the health centre; another building a short distance away which looked to be a house but turned out to be also a shop; and the little Orthodox Church and graveyard. That was the centre of Sevetti; the people it served were scattered up and down the lake and along the paths leading to it. One of the criticisms of the placing of the houses has been that they were too near to give proper feeding grounds for the reindeer, but too far apart to allow social life.

The graveyard looked unusual to an eye accustomed to the simple cross of the churches of the West. At the head of each grave was a wooden triangle on top of a straight piece of wood, with two strokes running across it at an angle.

As I walked back to the school I met one of the older teachers. He spoke to me in Finnish; I answered as best I could; and for a few minutes we carried on a sort of conversation. Then he broke off.

"You don't speak Finnish very well," he grumbled, and went off. I was hurt. Were their linguistic standards in Sevetti so high? It turned out later that he had mistaken me for the doctor. Fortunately no one else did. This sort of misunderstanding did arise from time to time; once a Swedish paper printed a hair-raising account of how difficult life was for the people of Inari commune in Finland since the dentist could hardly speak Finnish. I can only think that the reporter must have interviewed me over the telephone.

There were two teachers at the school at Sevetti, and one woman who combined the functions of health sister and midwife. They were Finns; it must have been an isolated life for them. Special allowances are, however, made to state and commune employees in these remote districts.

The Kolta Lapps came to Sevetti, which was nearest in character to their old Suonikylä, and something like their old way of life was re-established. That such a tiny group could have come to life again after the deluge is in itself a triumph. But the years away had affected them, particularly the younger ones, who appreciated the conveniences of civilization. If, too, a great deal is given to people—even if they need it and are in

some sense entitled to it—some of them come to feel that the
government should supply all that they require. The original
primitive community, isolated, knew that it had to look to itself
in the struggle with nature. The new community was an
artificial creation and could not avoid a sense that outside help
was available; and some of its members began to demand more
and more of the facilities which exist in the outside world.

Then the troubles began, because it is extremely expensive
to provide these facilities in such an inaccessible spot. A telephone line, for example, costs a good deal; a road far more; and
once a road is built the community is no longer isolated. It
then seems futile to have placed it in a place so difficult of
access. Sevetti is, therefore, a problem even to those most
anxious to preserve the Kolta Lappish way of life.

On our return journey we visited Partakko. This is another
school, remote, though not quite as remote as Sevetti, and on
the edge of Inari Lake. Here, in the middle of the wilderness,
totally removed from towns, villages, or indeed any other habitations at all, one finds a glisteningly modern school building.
It was not quite complete when we arrived; running water had
been installed, but electric light was still being fitted. A small
oil-driven generator was used for this.

We were taken to the teachers' room for coffee. It had modern
furniture, a white block ceiling and red and brown curtains.
An establishment like this has two teachers, one a man and one
a woman, sometimes quite young, who are jointly responsible
for the educational side of the school. One cannot help thinking with interest of the emotional effects of sharing such a
separated environment. A committee responsible for selecting
teachers was once regretting that they had only applications
from single men and women for a position which they thought
could be better filled by a married couple.

"Don't worry," said a prominent member of the committee.
"I'll soon get you a married couple," and he picked out a man
and woman of about the same age and sent them off to one of
these isolated schools. The effect can, however, sometimes be
in the opposite direction.

The visit to Partakko was only a short one, and after the
inspection had been completed we walked back to our plane.
I looked over my shoulder and saw the doctor in his black and
white Norwegian pullover walking along beside my wife. Suddenly there were shouts from the children following. They were
pointing to a little girl in their midst. They all crowded round
Arja and the doctor for a moment; there was a short, tense
pause, then the crowd opened up and I saw the girl spitting

blood, and a little white pearl on the sand. Another extraction had been performed.

We flew back in the fading light over a lake which looked like crinkled metal.

9 : *The Baby and the* Sauna

THE *sauna* is such an important feature of life in Finland, and so different from anything in the life of other countries, that it needs a chapter to itself. Every nation has its particular point of joy, a time in the week and an activity to which it looks forward: in Finland this is the *sauna*, a kind of bath, and the time is usually Friday or Saturday evening. In Lapland the effect of the *sauna* is greatest, for surely only in Lapland is the human body expected to stand a change of temperature from the boiling point of water down to twenty degrees Centigrade of frost—or more.

The *sauna* exists throughout Finland in different forms, private and public, but it is at its most picturesque in the country areas. There are, in Finland, between sixty and seventy thousand lakes; many are lonely pools with no one living there; others have perhaps one or two people in scattered dwellings round them; and others again, near the popular tourist centres, are thickly populated and have hotels within easy access.

One of the most typical sights in Finland, which could be seen at any of these places, is a tiny house built near the water's edge. It looks, from the outside, as though it might contain one room, or possibly two small ones, and has a porch at the front with a long seat facing the lake. It is, of course, of wood, and from its door a long pier of the same material runs into the lake, with at the end some steps going down into the water.

This is a *sauna*, and if it is in action its chimney will be smoking.

If you open the door you enter first a neat, plainly furnished room with a bench round the walls, a few clothes hooks, a table, and a mirror. This is the dressing room; here, if you are going to the *sauna*, you take your clothes off, and walk naked with bowl, soap and scrubbing brush through the second door which leads into the heart of the building.

There is usually a thermometer in this room, and it will probably be standing at between eighty and a hundred degrees Centigrade. It is quite possible that it may be as high as a hundred and ten, or well over boiling point. The effect of such heat is at first alarming: one feels it impossible to bear for more than a second or two. The first time I went into a *sauna* I thought that the hairs in my nostrils were being singed off.

Two things strike the eye in this main part of the *sauna*—a row of big wooden steps, perhaps a foot high and big enough to sit or lie on, and in one corner a metal oven with stones on top. Somewhere will be buckets or basins and in the middle of the floor an opening for water. This is one of the beauties of the *sauna*: there is no need to be afraid of splashing since all the surplus will go down the drain.

The English bath is a private occasion, but the *sauna* is essentially social. A certain time is set apart for men, and another for women, and usually several people go together. The first thing a Finn does on entering the hot part of the *sauna* is to take water in a metal scoop and throw it on to the hot stones above the oven. There is a hiss as the water is instantly vaporized and the steam rises. Those taking the *sauna* then spread themselves out on the steps, which go up nearly to the ceiling, and relax.

There is a considerable difference in temperature between floor and ceiling, so that one can, to some extent, control the fierceness of the effect. The heat soaks into the muscles and there is a wonderful feeling of comfort and harmony. The moisture on the surface of the body increases, being partly perspiration and partly condensation of the water vapour in the atmosphere, and one begins to think about going to wash.

Before doing this one often birches oneself. Stated baldly, this sounds horrifying; in practice it is very mild and pleasant. The birch whisks used are soft and leafy, producing no more than a pleasant tingling; a number of them are usually stored ready near the entrance, giving a clean woody fragrance to the air. After the birching and the washing comes the climax of the *sauna*, the sudden sharp descent into cold. One flings open the wooden door, rushes along the pier, and jumps into the lake.

This sudden extreme change of temperature is not, at first, noticed by the body as such: provided it has been sufficiently hot in the *sauna* the skin registers the water not as cold, but as caressing and velvety. Some cool themselves like this before washing, returning for further heat to the *sauna*. Enthusiasts do this as many as four times. After the *sauna* one rests for a while, gazing at the sunset from the porch if it is summer; then one drinks—for one is very thirsty—tea, coffee, fruit juice, or stronger drinks according to taste.

That is the country *sauna*. The town *sauna* is not so appealing, since usually in the town the dip in the lake must be replaced by a cold wash down. But in either country or town the *sauna* represents much more than a bath, much more even than a social occasion. It has, to the Finn, something positively spiritual about it: "After *sauna* one feels clean both inside and out." It also is a custom one must not interrupt; it would be fatal to arrange a social event on a night which people habitually reserved for *sauna*.

The *sauna* is also supposed to have beneficial effects on the health. "What tar, spirits and the *sauna* cannot cure," said the old Finns, "is beyond our power to deal with." I have, certainly, known a cold vanish after *sauna*, almost as though it had been sucked out; it felt also as though it had taken with it all my energy.

I went to my very first *sauna* before Arja and I were married. I had to go alone; and to walk naked into an entirely strange experience strips one of a considerable amount of self-confidence. This was one of the old type of smoke *sauna*, in which a fire is lighted in the *sauna* for some time, and the smoke is then allowed to escape through a hole in the roof before those using it go in. This is by some considered even better than the modern *saunas*. Unfortunately in this case the smoke had not properly escaped; I stumbled through a murky mist in which dim naked forms were wandering about, and thankfully emerged after the minimum possible time.

My second *sauna* was much pleasanter—in a country place by the side of a lake. What never occurred to me in those days, however, was that the *sauna* could become a regular part of the weekly routine, and what is perhaps most unusual for an Englishman—that I should experience it as a family affair. The basic *sauna* routine sets aside one period for men and another for women; but families with young children usually have a special time to themselves. For a long time in Ivalo we had no *sauna* of our own, and were hence dependent on the charity of kind friends.

The first such were Eetu and Maija, the chief officer of the commune and his wife. They lived in one of a number of flats in the same building as the commune offices; down in the basement was the *sauna*. Between three and four o'clock on a Saturday afternoon Arja and I would go along, taking with us a bag containing bath coats, soap, and scrubbing brushes. Usually Maija would greet us, then after a few minutes Eetu would come in dressed in a bath coat and with a cheery look in his eye. Our turn had arrived and we would dive down to the cellar and start on the operation. The cellar *sauna* in the commune offices was a good one, though not so romantic as the lakeside type; and from it one could not go to swim. We finished by sluicing ourselves down with as much cold water as seemed appropriate, dressing, then calling out in a loud voice as we went upstairs, "*Sauna vapaa!*" ("The *sauna's* free!"). Maija often gave us a bottle of fruit juice to drink down below and there was always tea waiting when we came up. One needs plenty of liquid after the *sauna* since so much of the body water has been lost in perspiration.

We frequently walked up the stairs to the flat in our bath coats and dressed up there.

Sometimes we went to the *sauna* owned by Henni, the chemist. This was a wooden building standing at the back of the chemist's shop. It was spacious inside, but unfortunately not very warm. One of the most elegant *saunas* was under the control of the chief forester, Martti Mäenpää, and his wife Helvi. From the back of the house in which he lived one walked across a small bridge and found the *sauna* standing like a little cottage just above the river. In the same building there lived an elderly woman who was under contract to do our washing. The *sauna* can serve more purposes than one; it is frequently used for laundry. In the past, in remote districts, children were frequently born in the *sauna*. It was the warmest place, the only place where hot water and privacy could be obtained, and the place which could most easily be cleaned. When the settlers returned to Lapland after the war, they built their *saunas* first and in some cases lived in them till the rest of the house was ready.

Some customs, which look perfectly natural when one is in one country, would seem very strange if transposed to another. It might, in England, give rise to some misunderstanding if one rang up a friend and said: "How about coming round for a bath on Saturday evening?" But in Finland an invitation to the *sauna* is quite a common form of social activity; and afterwards the party sit round and drink coffee, rosy-red, with towels round wet hair. Even the President gives and receives invitations to the *sauna*.

It was the family aspect of the *sauna*, however, which led to one of our big problems. One day when Lilian was a few months old, Arja said: "I think we ought to take Lilian to the *sauna*." I was taken aback at this idea; putting Lilian into that terrific temperature seemed almost as bad as allowing her to sleep outside in the freezing cold. Arja pointed out that most children went from a very early age. I felt extremely doubtful; it was a matter on which advice was difficult to obtain since most people in Lapland would have said: "Of course you should take the child to the *sauna*—mine went when they were far younger"—whilst most people in England would have looked on it as practically equivalent to murdering the girl.

Arja herself had some doubts, not having previously taken a young child to the *sauna*; she said that she would like to have someone there who was experienced in taking babies to *saunas*. I said firmly that one of the human rights a father possessed was to see what happened the first time his child went to the *sauna*; and this right I would by no means give up.

This resulted in a deadlock for some time. In the end, though with some nervousness, we simply took her along. We need not have worried; she accepted the *sauna* quite naturally. A young child may, indeed, find in the warmth of the *sauna* a pleasant reminder of its unborn life. For a child, too, there is a very pleasant freedom in this way of washing—it can play around with water, spill it on the floor, or tip the bowl over its head without anybody worrying.

Once she had been admitted to the *sauna* ceremonies, Lilian rapidly came to dominate them. She would be warmly wrapped up on a winter Saturday afternoon and placed on the *kelkka* —the little chair with runners—with the *sauna* equipment in a bag behind. The size of the bag seemed to have at least ·doubled since Lilian had joined the party. Then we would set off, one of us walking and the other pushing the *kelkka*, with Lilian's face peeping out of the red hat that went over her ears, and Lilian shouting at the top of her voice:

"*Saunaan! saunaan!*" ("To the *sauna*! to the *sauna*!").

Inside the *sauna*, the father of the child was expected to wash as quickly as possible and then stand by in the dressing room to receive his daughter. She came out pink and hygienic and was wrapped in her own bath coat with a special cap to cover the hair. She was then whisked off and dressed upstairs. That night she usually slept well.

In the coldest weather Lilian did not go to *sauna*; and below a certain temperature Arja herself would look doubtful.

"Do you think it is too cold to go today?" she would ask me, glancing at the thermometer which stood at minus twenty-five. But what could I answer? According to the traditions in which I had been brought up the effect of having a *sauna* at all should have been calamitous. It apparently was not, but I felt I could not weigh up the effect of any further changes in the conditions.

A woman is supposed to be at her most beautiful two hours after *sauna*. Unfortunately at that time she is usually putting her hair in pins.

10 : The Shadows Stretch Out

"Woe unto us! For the day goeth away, the shadows of the evening are stretched out."

Jeremiah vi, 4

"*Minä olen,*" I said. "I am."

"Good," said Arja. "Now you can speak Finnish."

That was a couple of days after we first met. Arja's remark was true, though misleading: it gave no indication of the immense amount of Finnish I could not speak. I quickly picked up a few useful words and phrases; then two difficulties appeared, the difficulties that confront almost any non-Finn who tries to study this language.

The first is the totally different character of Finnish. In most of the languages of Europe there are at least a few words which have some resemblance to English. Thus "electricity" said in different accents goes right across Europe: in Finland the word is *sähkö*, which has no similarity at all. Even Russian words, when extracted from the Cyrillic alphabet, occasionally have a familiar sound. Finnish is, however, not related to Russian; nor is it related to Swedish, nor to any other group of European languages except Estonian and Hungarian. It is supposed that these languages belonged to a group of people who came from behind the Ural mountains and swept round through Europe and into Finland, the Hungarian and Estonian groups dropping off on the way.

Estonian is closely connected with Finnish; Hungarian only distantly. The languages spoken by the Lapps are also related, but the difference is so great that no Finn would ever understand Lappish unless specially taught.

The second great stumbling block in learning Finnish is that not only the words, but also the whole structure of the language is completely different from English: instead of prepositions it uses a system of fourteen case endings. Thus "home" may be (amongst other things) *koti, kotiin* or *kotona*. This is peculiarly baffling to the beginner. Your ear picks out the word *kotona*. You reach for the dictionary and look it up. The dictionary has never heard of it. Or, on the other hand, you learn *koti*. You anxiously wait to hear someone say it: the word never comes.

The ending of a word also affects the internal structure: thus "man" is *mies*, but "for men" is *miehille*, and this is the word which is normally above the toilets.

The supreme torture, however, is provided by words which alter not only their endings but also their middles. Technically these are compound words: but how can one tell by looking at them? There is in Finland a town known as Uusikaupunki; but if you live in it you say Uudessakaupungissa, if you go to it you say Uuteenkaupunkiin, whilst on coming from it you must talk about Uudestakaupungista. I had thought that after a few months I should be able to speak Finnish fluently: I discovered that this was very far from the truth.

What was even more humiliating was that I found it difficult to keep up with my daughter. I had planned that I would study Finnish so that I always knew all the words that she did, and at the same time teach her English. This went quite well till she was around twenty months old, at which time she knew about twenty words of Finnish and the same number in English (though not the same words). Then, between the ages of two and three, her Finnish went up with a rush. It was like a tidal wave coming in; she knew words we had never heard anyone say in front of her; she seemed to pick them up from the very atmosphere. Finally she left me completely behind, so that one day—after having tried and failed to make me understand what she wanted—she said wearily:

"Don't you understand *anything* in Finnish?"

It is an interesting experience to be surrounded by a totally strange language and to be cut off entirely from native speakers of one's own. At first one thinks of this merely as a difficulty in communication; for the first month or two it is almost amusing; after a further time one realizes that one is being affected more deeply. A word is not simply the name of an object; it has subtle suggestions and associations not readily felt by people who are not native speakers of the language.

When one is surrounded with an unreadable language, too, one suddenly realizes the problems of life in modern civilization for the illiterate. One does not know which counter to use at the post office. One can never be certain that one has understood a timetable. One suddenly sees a sign saying:

*Huom! Ei ole auki maanantaina.**

What does it mean? It may be of supreme importance or quite insignificant. It may say something entirely trivial that you don't even want to know or it may order all foreigners to be out of the country by Monday. You don't think it is anything

* Notice: NOT OPEN ON MONDAY.

very bad, but you can't be quite certain. Then again, you can't read the news. You may be told it, but that is not the same: so much depends on inflections of the voice, on what is put in and what is left out.

When we went to Lapland I had known that we should be going to a strange environment; I had assumed that this would have the effect of drawing us closer together. What I had not realized was that Arja, Finnish-speaking, would be part of the environment whilst I was not. It was as though we had been put into solution: one of us had dissolved into it whilst the other had been left, isolated.

Children from Lappish-speaking homes, who are compelled by law to go to school when they are seven—often boarding school—and who are usually taught by Finnish teachers in Finnish, also meet some of these problems.

As the summer fled away and the autumn ended I learnt something of the emotional effects of the Lapland climate. I had thought that the first winter in Lapland would be the worst; to my surprise the second winter was much more difficult. The first winter had been so novel, so far removed from previous experience that it had been simply exciting. That winter, too, I had thought would be the only one we should spend in Lapland. The very fact that we were there showed that our plans had changed. In London I had been told by the examiners that they would grant me an M.Sc. on what I had already done; or I could go back and work for a further period in order to get a doctor's degree. I took the cash in hand; the research work now seemed like a trail which I had followed too far; there was no point in spending further time on it as I was no longer going in that direction; I had made a break with the old life.

I did not fully appreciate, when I left England, the exact step I was taking. I had known that my life was not satisfactory; yet I might have allowed it to go on in the same way through not seeing clearly how to change it. In Lapland, amongst a different set of values, I realized I could not go back to my former pigeon-hole. To go forward, whatever the cost to me or other people, would be less than the price of giving in.

It would be nice to pretend that the move to Lapland had been a carefully planned step and that I saw exactly where I was going to go. It was not; it was more like finding oneself in the wrong train and jumping out into the forest, landing bruised, confused, and not at all sure where one was, but feeling it better to wander through the trees till one found the right path rather than wait for another wrong train. Sometimes, I think, one has to make a jump like this; the vision will not clarify until one is outside the old situation.

Changing horses in midstream may not be a safe or politically advisable move; but it teaches one a great deal both about horses and about streams. Unfortunately at the moment when one is between one horse and the other one is in an extremely helpless position. It is an awkward moment and becomes increasingly painful the longer it lasts. My awkward moment was a long one. What was the new way to step out?

I had had three possibilities in mind when I went to Lapland, all connected with writing. The first was for a technical book; I put this aside fairly soon. To do that one needed to sink in to the subject in a place where technical reference sources were easily available. That was not Lapland. The second was for a book about Lapland itself; I was gathering material for this continuously, but knew it would be some time before I could write it.

The third was a novel. It had been begun before I left England; I had expected to finish it during the first year; in practice it took much longer. I did not know what it would lead to; I did not know whether it would ever be published; but before I could go any further that book had to be finished. It was part of the working out of a struggle in my own mind. But . . . the moments of darkness when one cannot see the way ahead at all and thinks one is simply a complete fool who might now be in a comfortable job . . . with a pension!

In those autumn and early winter months I was particularly conscious of the spirit and atmosphere of the country; and, cast adrift from the old moorings, I was less protected from the underlying primitive forces than those who had a familiar routine job each day.

The summer had been so incredibly full of light that it seemed as though darkness had vanished for ever. As one sat at midnight looking at the prolific landscape with the sun moving horizontally along the horizon one just could not believe that the white, concealing, night-covered winter scene had ever existed or was going to exist again. Slowly, at first, so that one hardly noticed, and then with lightning rapidity, as though one were falling down a precipice—the summer vanished. The evenings were cooler, one noticed; it was even a little dark at midnight; and at first one felt cheated, as though one had been promised the sun for ever, night and day, and now as if it were being taken away.

Then one saw that the nights were becoming rapidly longer and the day darker as though a great bird were spreading its wings over the sky. One wanted to resist it—to clutch at the daylight, source of all life, which was vanishing; and one realized that this was impossible, the darkness was inevitably coming, that no human effort could stop it, that one was condemned.

Echoes of primitive superstition and dread awoke: the sun was leaving us, life was dying, perhaps it would never come back. Looking at those wild flaming sunsets of autumn and watching that golden circle disappearing one understood how a northern people could conceive the idea of the twilight of the gods—the vanishing of the powers which drove the universe; and one was gripped with desire to live life to its fullest, to exhaust oneself with the summer, then abandon hope and plunge into darkness with the sun.

It struck at some of the most fundamental ideas, this loss of the sun, at the basic securities one had believed in since childhood. "While the earth remaineth, seedtime and harvest . . . day and night shall not cease." Could the writer of that have used such words if he had lived in the north? For now day was failing; the sun, ultimate symbol of regularity to almost everyone in the world, could no longer be relied on; and primitive man, who feared that the sun might not come back, seemed as profound as the modern who assumes that he is quite safe and that it will.

There is a time in Lapland when the sun has almost gone and yet the snow has not firmly arrived. It is the darkest time of the year. The sky is dark, the earth is dark; and during this time the incidence of mental troubles and suicides is greatest. At this time of the year and also at the change of season in the spring I sometimes suffered from migraine: bright circles and spots in front of my eyes and for a short time blind patches. It never lasted long, and it nearly always came at these particular times of the year. Once or twice, as I walked across the bridge, I looked at the dark waters below: for a second they had a wicked attraction. I walked on and the sudden impulse disappeared.

"No man is an island unto himself. . . ." We are connected by innumerable tiny threads with the society in which we are brought up; it is only when these are cut that we realize what strength we draw from them.

Lilian in the snow at winter-
time trying out her first skis

After the last patient has gone
Arja sorts out her instruments

Inari Church

Paavo Pandy's store for hay

Our reindeer at Pandy's; Arja is on the left, and the reindeer man on the right

THEN the snow came. I stood at the window and watched it falling steadily and rhythmically down, flake after flake dropping on to the dead landscape, transforming it into its winter form. The world of the sun had gone, but a new world was being born. It exercised an almost hypnotic effect, this steadily, inexorably falling snow; and through it one could hear the soft melancholy clanging of the bell as a horse went past dragging a sledge with big dark-green cubes of fodder on it. In earlier days Lapland produced enough foodstuffs for its own animals in winter. Now these have to be imported from the south, and the sleighs would drive up to Taka Lappi and Osuuskauppa—those multiple stores which provided almost everything for man and beast—and then back to their farms.

Then the *kelkkas* appeared, the "chairs on runners" which cost about a pound and were both the playthings of the children and a swift and economical means of transport. Often a dark-clothed woman would be behind one, with one foot on a runner and the other kicking vigorously at the smooth snow; and in front on the seat a Lapland child, plump in its winter wrappings, or a big shopping bag, or both.

The snow-removal machines went along the roads; the one with the bar at the front which shoved the snow off and piled it at the sides, irritating me by constantly leaving a heap across the bottom of our path; then the snow plough, with its scoops, which cleared off the loose stuff remaining. The first was slow and thoughtful, working in a steady methodical way; but the second flew along the roads with dash and devilment. Sometimes it would swoop round a complete circle in the centre of Ivalo with almost Gallic abandon. At night, with its lights on, it looked like a red and gold insect. Finally, there was the Bear: this had a metal rake at the back with which it tore lines along the surface of the road, reducing the chances of skidding.

The bicycles still kept on, and so did the motor-cyclists, but the latter now had skids on their feet. On London roads one is almost certain to get knocked down by a motor vehicle, but walking along the road in Ivalo and hearing a swish behind, you did not know what might hit you: horse, reindeer, *kelkka*, ski-er, car, snow plough, or snow bus. It was a world of infinite possibility.

The winter life of Ivalo had begun. The northern lights were now showing; the first winter I had rushed out every time a scrap of them was visible and even made detailed observations; this second winter I became a little indifferent, only going out for an exceptionally fine exhibition. The river froze over, and the snow ploughs went down the middle of it, making an excellent winter road. The walk from our house to the school was shortened by fifteen minutes; we could now go straight across the river instead of round by the bridge. There was a steep bank on the other side, and this was usually a mass of parked skis and *kelkkas*.

People mixed freely in Ivalo; the shortest way to unpopularity would have been to have given yourself airs. They would have delighted in taking down anyone they thought set himself above them. When a very important person—very important indeed—came to Lapland and wanted to drive a reindeer they related joyfully how they chose the wildest reindeer, which upset him in the snow. Kalle was regarded as a good *nimismies* because he would have a drink with the men; he knew his people and they could talk to him without formality.

There were, nevertheless, undoubted social groupings. One group, consisting of professional people and business men, included the *nimismies*, the doctor, Gunnar, who owned the saw mill, one or two commune officials, Henni the chemist, Martti the chief forester, Captain Juha (and his wife) who commanded the frontier guards stationed a mile or two outside Ivalo, and one or two others. One of the great pillars of social life in Finland is the coffee party, which can be held at any time of the day or night. We drank a great deal of coffee with the members of this group.

From time to time a dance would be held in the Maja, the local hotel. This was often in aid of some good cause. The first we ever went to was organized by *Sotilas Kotinaiset*; literally, soldiers' home women. This existed to improve the furnishings and other amenities with which the accommodation of military organizations was provided. Sometimes the music was provided by a band in which the leading salesman from the Taka Lappi stores worked hard, at other times by records which I came to know note for note. Most of the dances were the usual modern type, not very spectacularly performed; but occasionally a *jenkka*, a traditional dance, would be played. Into this the company would fling themselves with abandon, as though it had reached some secret spring of vitality.

There was a good deal of steady drinking during these affairs, but none of the men in the above group ever got very drunk on these occasions. With hardly any exceptions, however, they never went home in their own cars.

There was no reason why anyone who wanted should not come into the first-class section of the Maja; but not everyone did, and not everyone could afford it. The less well-off younger unmarried people went to the Red House, a building of this colour which stood some distance off the main road not very far from the post-office. Here cheaper non-alcoholic dances were held. The Red House also became a cinema twice a week, which, since it was the only cinema, was very democratic: everyone who wanted to see a film had to come here. As a cinema the Red House had two defects: its seats were not soft and it only possessed one projector. In the middle of some tropical love scene the lights would go up to reveal the dark clothes of the people we knew so well, reminding us that we were not in some distant corner of the world but at home in Ivalo. I wondered if people in the tropics were ever returned abruptly to reality in this way whilst watching a film of Lapland.

The Maja also had a second restaurant, furnished much more plainly and less expensively than the first-class one; this appealed to those who wanted to drink but were not anxious to spend so much. The dancing space was, however, common to both, and my dancing usually followed a fixed pattern: out through the door of the first-class restaurant, past the band, into the other restaurant, turn sharply where the tables started, underneath the picture of Kaapin Jouni—a famous Lapp— and so back again. Though there are more men than women in Lapland, this was never very obvious in Ivalo as for much of the time many of the men were away, either in the forest or with the reindeer. A number of unmarried men doing work of this sort who had come in to Ivalo for a short time would usually be in this second section of the Maja.

Social life in Ivalo, however, was not confined to the Maja and the Red House. It also included the school. This was a block of buildings standing on the opposite side of the river to the house in which we lived. The buildings were modern; indeed, some complained that this very modernity unfitted the Lappish children for their own kind of life. It was really three schools in one: an elementary school, a secondary school, and a continuation school. All children who did not go to the secondary school had to go to the continuation school. This was the only one of its kind in the commune, which meant that every child in the commune had to spend a period in Ivalo. Most of them lived at the school during this time, in a separate residential block. The teachers also had flats round the school: it formed, therefore, a kind of educational colony.

The school had a good hall which was used for social functions: the Independence Day ceremonies were held there. We have, of course, no Independence Day in England, and I had no idea how one celebrated Independence Day; I thought it would be an occasion for light-heartedness and rejoicing.

In this I was misled by my wife. "Come to the Independence Day party," she said. Unfortunately she has never understood clearly the exact significance we attach to the word "party" and uses it for almost any kind of meeting. I went, dressed in my lightest, most carefree suit: and found the hall filled with a solemn, black-suited audience and something close to a religious ceremony about to begin.

For many people in Ivalo, however, most of life centred round home; perhaps a small home, sometimes a minute home, but often a home which they owned and sometimes which they had built themselves. Our neighbour, who was a carpenter, lived in one of these tiny wooden houses with his wife and three children. It was the sort of house in which an ordinary family in Lapland might live; it had one room and a kitchen; and to me it was a miracle that so much could be compressed into so little space, or that it could possibly look so tidy when housing little Pekka with the big brown eyes and his older sister and brother.

Nearly all the people we met were heart-warmingly friendly to us in their different ways.

There was one other force working in Ivalo, however, which had a profoundly dividing effect. The Lutheran Church claims ninety-six per cent of the population of Finland as its members. This is, however, in many cases purely nominal, since the Church acts as a registrar and one must either belong to this or some other recognized church or apply to be put on the civil list.

One sect within the Lutheran Church which is particularly strong in Lapland takes an extreme position. Its members must not smoke, drink, dance, or even listen to music unless it is serious and preferably religious music. They regard the Lutheran Church as having wandered away from its original principles; they are the "faithful", the only ones who have really found salvation.

The members of this sect are called the Laestadians; the sect was founded in the middle of last century by Lars Leevi Laestadius, a Lutheran pastor, and swept through Lapland. It is said to have had a pronounced effect in restraining excessive drinking at that time.

The movement has one striking feature, a feature which antagonizes many: at times the "saved" go into a frenzy, shouting, weeping, flinging their arms about and jumping up and down. It may well be that this does provide a relief which others obtain in different and perhaps more harmful ways. But it is the sort of practice which tends to create sharp division: those not in it are apt to be repelled by it. The Laestadians formed a group within the Ivalo Church, and there was often opposition between it and the other members. The Laestadians worked for the appointment of pastors with their own views, and in any group to which they belonged they had a strong influence.

That October we started the Ivalo English Society. I had some idea of teaching English when we first went to Ivalo, and had already done a little; the possibility of forming a group interested in studying England and the English language so much farther north than could be expected appealed to me. There are a number of Finnish–British societies in Finland, but the majority of them are in the more industrial south and none before had arisen north of the Arctic Circle. There were about half a dozen people in Inari commune who could speak English fairly well, perhaps as many more who knew a little, and a few thousand who would have denied any knowledge of the language.

We told a few people—the way information normally gets round in Lapland—that there would be a meeting at our house, and about twenty came along. Later this was to increase to over forty. A teacher at the continuation school, Ulla Hauhia, became secretary, and we started classes at three different levels. Our founder members included several of the teachers; Eetu, the chief executive of the commune, and his wife; Inkeri, the pretty pharmacist; one or two people from the bank, amongst them the sister of Miss Junttila (who had worked for my wife in the surgery) and who was, also like her sister, noticeably well dressed; Sirkka, the wife of Kalle the *nimismies*, and Helvi, the wife of Martti the chief forester, and a number of workers from Osuuskauppa, the shop, and later from the post office. It cut across the divisions both of religious opinions and of politics.

Some of those who came knew no English at all. Teaching one's own language to those who do not speak it is one of the most fascinating of all forms of teaching. Results are so clear; if at the beginning they know nothing and after six months they begin to say a few phrases, you know definitely that you have achieved this amount of success. You do not, as in some other forms of teaching and in research, have to wait five, ten or twenty years to see whether the work has benefited humanity or not; and with this goes the thrill of establishing communication where it had not existed before.

It is also good practice in teaching: you must know each step that you are going to take before you begin to teach, and some knowledge of the language of those being taught is a very great help. My own acquaintance with Finnish by this time was, as Mr. Weller would have said, various and peculiar. It was based on a book for American soldiers; a close study of the baptismal service, made when my daughter was christened; a number of medical and dental words; and a selection of phrases connected with babies. It sufficed, however, to put me in touch with the class.

Fetsi, our Kolta Lappish helper, also joined the beginners' group and appeared to be quite receptive to English. Lapps have one advantage in learning English. The Finnish language does not possess any sound corresponding to the English "th" sound as in "this". Such a sound is therefore usually not easy for Finns to make. This kind of sound does, however, exist in Lappish, and Lapps can therefore more easily form it when speaking English.

Of those who denied all knowledge of English, some undoubtedly possessed a latent ability to speak a little. This came out under the influence of alcohol; men who had previously not said a word of English would after a few drinks produce the most unexpected phrases. I was out for a walk one day when I saw two men in a car by the side of the road. I knew one of them quite well; he had a business in Ivalo. He had never shown any signs of speaking anything but Finnish. But now he did. He beckoned me over and waved a bottle.

"My good friend," he said. "My good friend. It is a little—" he wanted to say "party", but here his English failed him, so he flung in a German word—"It is a little *fest*." And he insisted on giving me a drink. It was at least encouraging to know that the underlying feelings towards the English released by alcohol were of this kind and not the opposite.

At times it was necessary to walk carefully in the English

society. There were in it both Laestadians, with their special outlook, and those with broader views. In the same group there might be a Laestadian who objected to any kind of alcohol and a girl who acted as a waitress at the Maja, the hotel, and much of whose work consisted in serving drinks; and one wanted to give both the sort of English they needed. The Laestadians were, however, good students; and provided their susceptibilities were not offended they were quite ready to enjoy themselves at the social events.

These culminated with a Christmas party at Törmänen, a school on the main road a few miles south of Ivalo. This was held at the beginning of December, when Finns hold what they call *pikku Joulu*, "little Christmas"—a prelude to the main celebrations which are to follow. I had suggested plum pudding as a suitable English Christmas dish, but on this point I was overruled and instead we ate the traditional Finnish Christmas food—rice pudding. I have never been able to feel the same enthusiasm for rice that I feel for plum pudding; I only took one helping, which upset those who had prepared it, and they asked me anxiously what was wrong. But they enjoyed the *pikku Joulu*; Eetu laughed till the tears ran down his face, and the rest relaxed in a way which showed that Finns could get rid of their inhibitions even without alcohol. Outside the world was filled with Christmas trees and covered with snow: the world of the Christmas cards, yet our world—here— real. Not very far away from our party was, according to the Finns, the home of Father Christmas himself—Korvatunturi— the "Ear Hill" from which he listens to what is going on in the world.

One other social event that winter had in it a certain amount of regret: a final party we held for Jaakko, the tall commune secretary, and his wife Liisi. They had recently had a second child; only very cramped living accommodation could be found for them in Ivalo, little more than a room and a kitchen, so they were leaving for the south. This party was held in the Maja, and attended by about eight or ten of the professional group. Looking round that group, they divided up into two: those who had come to Lapland for a year or two, and who would go back again; and those who would never leave. Some of the men would say, jokingly, that it would be impossible for them to go anywhere else; they had stayed too long in Lapland. Five years, they said, was the maximum time: after that you couldn't work anywhere else. Generally the men didn't mind the idea; Lapland suited them; but their wives were not so certain.

It was a serious thought, this, that some could not leave Lapland; and yet, if there had not been so many forces drawing me back, if I could have put down more solid roots there—I might have stayed.

WEST of the Ivalo–Inari road lies a region of lakes, hills, and rivers in which there are very few inhabitants. It stretches right across into Norway; and to get into it usually involves rough travelling. The river and lake chains, stretching south-west to north-east, are one way; but from Inari village at least one road negotiable by car enters these wilds. This road goes to Menes-järvi, which is a lake, and at the time we were in Lapland the road stopped there, almost as though it had reached a frontier.

We went to Menesjärvi at the beginning and end of the second winter, first in the autumn and the second time in the spring. I had been told that Menesjärvi was a Lappish village. In my ignorance I assumed that a Lappish village might look something like an English one—with houses grouped round some kind of centre. I knew enough by this time not to expect a church, since there were only two churches in normal use throughout the commune.

What I still did not understand was the difference in the Lappish idea of what constituted distance—of the Lappish meaning of "near". This is illustrated by the following story. Arja asked one of her Lappish patients if the houses in this woman's village were far apart.

"Oh no," said the patient. "They're right on top of one another. Only three miles between them."

Arja went to Menesjärvi first, together with Miss Junttila and the portable dental equipment. I followed a day or two later in one of the Ivalo taxis. The taxi turned left just before reaching the centre of Inari village, along a stony, winding, narrow road that led towards the forest. It ran between the hills, curving away from the river which flows into the Inari Lake, but later curving back to touch the lake from which the river comes, the Solojärvi. It was not gloomy country, but it was very lonely.

We went on like this for between one and two hours; then the road suddenly dwindled to a footpath and we decided that we had come too far. We turned round, went back, and found a track going off to the left; half a mile or so along this we came to a steep hill, with the lake at its foot and a little to the right a school building: a very clean, new-looking school, with a boat on the beach in front of it and children outside, arrested in what they were doing by the sound of the car. This was Menesjärvi school, where we were to stay; but where was the village? I looked round for it, perplexed; at length I managed to find one house, not very far from the school. For the rest, there seemed nothing but lake and wooded shore. It was only later that I discovered other houses, tucked into odd corners of the woods where they met the water.

This was no village in the English sense; if it had any centre, it was the lake itself. A Lappish "village" is frequently a loose, far-flung structure, with the houses not even within sight of each other.

It was a very modern school; it had only recently been completed. It had pleasant classrooms, electric light and running water, and flush toilets (at least for the teachers). Standing by the side of the blue lake with the sun lighting up the russet trees round it and the light reflected from its unspotted surface, the school looked like a creative triumph—civilization brought to the wilderness. Yet there hung about it the faintest possible air of uneasiness.

The school stood at the farthest limit which one culture— our culture, the culture of the machine—had reached. Up to that point one could go (at least in summer) by car, by the normal methods of transport. Behind it lay overcrowded cities and towns and the whole business of organized living in the way of London or Helsinki or New York. Ahead, one had to change. One could no longer go by car: one must walk or take a boat or in winter go by reindeer. Ahead were people who lived by fishing and reindeer keeping, widely separated from each other and little touched by the machine: a different culture, a culture closely linked with nature.

Back in Ivalo the machine culture was strong enough to seem the culture of the future, strong enough to be indifferent to criticism. Here, in Menesjärvi, it was not so clear. The school sprang out of the machine culture and, largely, its teaching was designed to fit children for the ordinary Finnish way of life, since the subjects were the same as those in any other Finnish school. But the children here belonged to the other culture; they were Lappish children; and all around it were the Lapps living their own kind of life. So the school was like a fruit at the end of a long stalk connecting it with the way of life from which it sprang; a fruit in a region where it was regarded as a little strange, where its right to exist was not entirely unchallengeable.

Arja was still at work when I arrived. She had converted a small room on the ground floor of the school into a temporary surgery; two children were waiting outside with an expression of resigned melancholy. At that time, the portable drill was of the human-powered foot-operated type, and Miss Junttila was working this. She looked as though she would have fitted in well in some previous existence to a spinning wheel. Both Arja and Miss Junttila looked tired; they had been working very long days.

The school was run, as far as teaching was concerned, by a married couple in their late twenties: Maija-Liisa* and Matti. Both had first taught on the western side of Lapland; it was there that they had met. Though cut off from some facilities, a teacher in Lapland does have a number of compensations; usually he or she has good living accommodation. Maija-Liisa and Matti had a comfortable three-roomed flat, centrally heated, and which also possessed a fireplace.

This fireplace proved very useful later in the evening. As the sun was setting we went out with Matti in the boat to inspect his nets which were stretched across the lake. He had a good catch; we took this back and lit the fire in the fireplace. We could have fried the fish in a conventional frying pan in the kitchen. The fire was there, however, flaring up the chimney and lighting up our faces with a volatile red glow. So we sat round and cooked the fish by holding it near the flames, a way simple but producing an exceptionally appetizing result.

Besides Arja, Miss Junttila and myself, the doctor was also visiting Menesjärvi and had brought with him two nurses. In the morning, since there was considerable pressure on the running water, I decided to have my shave in the lake. It was the coldest shave I ever had; and the one with the most colourful background. A sharp wind was dragging little waves on to the shore; a birch leaned out over the water, its yellow flaring up against the blue beneath it and the dark pines in the distance. The hills ran along behind, with tree-serrated edges; further away, higher mountains stood out in a gentle purple. Near me was a little reddish peninsula of sand; the sun turned the red to a bright gold where it touched the water. Here and there was a light dusting of snow.

From where I stood there was no trace visible of anything made by mankind, nothing but the vast display of nature. Primitive man might have stared at the same scene. Looking at it gave a feeling of satisfaction, of cleanliness: as though one were seeing a picture from which the dust had been brushed away. Though I did not realize it at the time, these great,

* These hyphenated first names are common in Finland.

uninhabited, natural landscapes had a permanent effect; they left behind a lurking nostalgia for them. They made the rest of Europe overcrowded, so that however beautiful the surroundings somewhere else, one thought: "Attractive, yes; but not very far away is the road and I am almost certain to meet other people soon. In Lapland there would be nothing but untouched nature, and if I wanted I could go all day and be alone with it." Anywhere else there would be a slight feeling of irritation, of resentment that an over-regulated society was so near. Perhaps it is this faint irritation which is at the basis of so-called "Lapland madness"—the haunting desire to return again to Lapland, from which some find it impossible to escape.

It struck at something, too, in my earlier life. I had never been able to escape from a queer dissatisfaction with the circumstances in which I found myself; and to quieten it I had developed secret gigantic ambitions. Now in Lapland I began to wonder if that had really been the answer; perhaps that dissatisfaction had been a longing for something life-giving which our society did not provide. In Lapland it seemed foolish to be so ambitious; one could there believe in a life which aimed not so much to progress as to be vividly conscious of existence for its own sake, to be in harmony with the universe instead of trying to conquer it.

Not everyone is affected in this way by Lapland: some people could barely stand a week of it.

We sent most of the equipment back by taxi, and ourselves returned by the river route. The party set out across the lake in a couple of rowing boats. Knowing how cold it could be on the water, I had put on a couple of thick pullovers; but it was a vigorous row and by the time we had travelled two miles or so to the far side of the water I was perspiring freely. We set off on a four-mile walk through the forest: an attractive walk, but the party seemed determined to show how fast it could go and there was little time to look around. It was as much as I could do to get one of my pullovers off. The path eventually came to a river; there was a wooden house in a cleared space by the side of it, and here we stopped.

The river was the Lemmenjoki; the name means "river of love". It rose some thirty miles to the south-west. Further up it was possible to pan gold, though the quantities obtained were very limited. Kalle once showed us a small piece which had come from this region. About eighty years ago, however, there was a miniature gold rush and traces of it are still visible. It is said that although the gold was sent through the post in packets quite simply wrapped up, and although it was known that gold was in the packets, none of it was ever stolen. Certainly in my own experience Lapland was a very honest place.

There were two rooms in the wooden house; we went into one of them and a woman started to make coffee for us. A small boy sat on the far side with his arm round a big dog and watched us in the shy, silent way Lappish children have. Opposite, across the river, we could see another house: this had belonged to one of the wealthiest and best-known Lapps—Kaapin Jouni, now dead, whose picture was in the Ivalo Maja. Where so few people live, the houses are generally known by the names of their owners.

Coffee over, we got into a boat—this time with a motor—and started off down the river. Soon, however, we had to get out. A narrow stretch of water had to be negotiated and the boat could not get past it with so many passengers. Only Alli Junttila was allowed to remain; as we climbed the steep bank she floated away in the gorge between the two sharply rising sides like a queen in her royal barge. We rejoined the boat round a bend in the river and travelled thus for some distance, getting out and walking at intervals.

With its sharply rising banks, still waters reflecting the shapes of the trees, and broad, ever-varying curves where it swirled into light out of a tree-shadowed gloom and then back into dimness again, the Lemmenjoki was a very attractive river; but it was very cold. I was also hungry; Finns possess an ability to go all day without food if they feel like it, an ability which I do not share. I found it increasingly difficult to appreciate the beauty of the journey, and more and more wanted a cup of coffee. Eventually we stopped and went into a small house by the river.

Inside a woman was baking; two children were playing round her. Here occurred a tragedy of non-communication. The woman seemed rather quiet; we thought that this was due to lack of enthusiasm at having her home invaded by total strangers, as is apt to happen to houses on these lonely routes. Some time afterwards, however, she came to Ivalo to Arja's surgery as a patient. She had been quiet that afternoon, she said, because she had been suffering badly from toothache: she had not known who we were, and had been longing for us to go. Had she only breathed a word of her trouble she could have had an almost—for Lapland—unprecedented assembly of technical skill to deal with it: a doctor, a nurse, a health sister and an engineer as well as the dentist.

After a short break we went on again in the boat, and as

evening was coming reached Paadarjärvi, a broad lake into
which the river ran; then, finally, we slid down the channel
joining Paadarjärvi to the last lake, Solojärvi, and with hardly
any light left touched the far side where the Inari–Menesjärvi
road ran and a car was waiting for us. In those last two lakes the
cold bit into me with icy teeth. After the vigorous exertion of
the row and the walk, the long chilly hours with very little
possibility of motion had had a bad effect and for a few days
afterwards I was in bed with a temperature. This contrast of
conditions struck me as much more trying physically than any
of the winter ones.

It was winter when we made our second trip to Menesjärvi;
or, rather, at the very end of the winter when the snow still
remained but was getting very soft, and spring was expected
any day. The road was closed and there were only two possible
ways of getting there—by plane, landing on skis; or by reindeer. We planned to go by the first and return by the second.
The seaplane in which we had gone to Sevetti had seemed tiny
beside even the smallest international plane; but it looked big
in comparison with the little silver shape which was waiting
for us on the frozen lake of Inari one April day. It held two
people, or at the most three, besides the pilot.

The pilot was ready for us and as soon as we were inside he
slammed the door and the plane began bumping over the
frozen snow with increasing speed. He had, when we spoke to
him on the telephone, been doubtful about taking off at all
due to the bad condition of the snow; eventually he said it
might be possible either at dawn or just before it was dark. So
here we were, rushing across the snow on Inari Lake late in
the afternoon, with my mind suddenly vividly aware of all that
had been said of the difficulties of taking off.

The bumping increased, then all at once the pilot pulled
back the stick and we were circling around the village of Inari,
a few dark shapes of houses and the long road marked out
against the white and black pattern of the snow and the trees.
We were flying very low, and to our right the bare white top of
a hill rose high above us. Compared with the planes used by
the major airlines, there was so little between us and the air
that one might have been a disembodied spirit.

I asked the pilot where the plane came from. "Don't talk to
him," hissed Arja from the back seat. The pilot turned round
and assured her that it was all right. He said that the plane
came from the British, who bought it from the Americans at
the beginning of the last war.

I sincerely hoped the British had been careful with it.

Down below and to the right I could see long oval gaps between the trees, frozen lakes connected by thin white ribbons where the rivers had run. I tried to identify Paadarjärvi and Solojärvi, though this was more difficult than might have been expected: one could not be certain what was a frozen lake and what was a clearing in the trees. In a few moments, however, we were over Menesjärvi: it was impossible to mistake the school building.

As we landed, the children came running out to meet us, blue and red flashing over the snow. A group of children in Lapland always seem gaily coloured. Looking closely one sees that not all are wearing Lappish clothing, indeed that only few have the full dress, boots, and headgear; but all have at least one touch of colour and the cumulative effect is striking. The red Lappish caps are the principal ingredient; by themselves they give a vivacious note to any group. They were worn not only by the Lapps but also by many women in Ivalo, including Arja, Lilian and several of our friends.

Some of the children were being taken back to Inari by the plane; they scrambled in laughing, without any inhibitions about the machine. After a moment or two it took off and the group below waved and shouted as their colleagues disappeared towards Inari.

We walked up to the flat in which Maija-Liisa and Matti lived in the school. It was now nearly the end of the winter and supplies were beginning to run short. They were mostly brought into Menesjärvi before the road was closed, and after that it was difficult to get anything, at least in large quantities. Whilst we were there we had a little milk; but this involved Matti in a ski trip of some fifteen miles to get it. Letters were brought by reindeer; there was a regular postal service once a week.

I wondered what it would be like to live here through the winter. Besides Maija-Liisa and Matti there would be the woman who looked after the living arrangements of the children (called *täti* or "aunt"), the cook, the caretaker, and one or two helpers, virtually shut up together for several months. I decided that I could stand it for one winter but not more. To live there longer the basis of one's life would need to be outside—one would need to follow the reindeer or be keenly interested in fishing through the ice. For outside, in Lapland, one is free and unbounded, one's feet are in a large place; but inside life moves within a narrow circle.

We had some of our meals with the schoolchildren. They were very quiet, all suddenly rising at the end and saying together, *"Kiitos, Jeesus, ruuasta"* ("Thank you, Jesus, for food"). Meals in Lapland schools gave me a certain amount of trouble since I am not a good organizational type and invariably seemed to have half my meal still in front of me and my mouth full when the moment came to rise. Outside the children seemed much more relaxed; they played at throwing a lassoo and a game in which they stood round in a circle and ran up and down lines going to the centre, the one in the middle trying to catch the others.

Maija-Liisa pointed out one or two children who looked different from the rest. She said they were the children of Finnish mothers and German fathers, the Germans who had been there during the war. Finland was never an occupied country during the last war, and for most of the time the Germans were not enemies, so there is no suggestion that the relationships were anything but voluntary.

Maija-Liisa herself was something of an enigma. She spoke both English and French; in her student days she had spent a year in Paris. We played her collection of French records in the evenings. She did not particularly enjoy the Lapland outdoor sports, such as ski-ing; yet she said that she loved Menesjärvi and did not want to leave it.

Some of the children, said Maija-Liisa, came to school with very little knowledge of what it was like; one boy had never eaten a hen's egg. Most of them lived at the school, some going home at week ends, others not till the end of the term.

One Lapp who carried considerable weight in affairs lived close by. He was Erkki Jomppanen. in his early thirties, leader of the *paliskunta*—that is to say, responsible for the arrangements in one reindeer-breeding area—and in addition chairman of the Inari Council. He had also carried on business as a merchant both in Inari and Menesjärvi. We went to call on him one evening; as chairman of the council he was concerned with the work of the Inari commune dentist, namely Arja.

He lived in a wooden house on the edge of the lake, five minutes away from the school. It was simply but comfortably furnished and possessed the one telephone in Menesjärvi. Before we left he went away for a minute and came back with something in his hand—a gift for Lilian. It was a reindeer-skin cap, beautifully soft since it was made from the skins of reindeer which had died young, a rare and expensive material.

The Lapps who lived round Menesjärvi belonged to one or other of the two larger Lappish groupings; they would have considered themselves as something quite different from the Kolta Lapps. Some of the other Lapps were, indeed, critical of the Kolta Lapps and thought that they had received more assistance in proportion and more attention than the others. Three groupings were commonly spoken of: Kolta Lapps, Inari Lapps, and *tunturi*—hill Lapps. Each spoke a different variety of Lappish; but that spoken by the *tunturi* Lapps, Northern Lappish, extended the farthest, being spoken also in Norway and Sweden.

We now began to organize our journey back: this we had determined should be by reindeer. There was a prolonged discussion as to what we should do. The post reindeer came at intervals but we should have to wait for them and they were slow—the journey took eight hours. A neighbour on the other side, about a mile away, had some faster reindeer and might take us. We went ski-ing over the snow—now decidedly sticky —to see him. He wasn't in; his wife said she would ask him. Later on that day he sent a message to say that the snow was almost too soft for the reindeer to travel and why didn't we go by plane which was so easy and anyway would only cost about the same? This severely economic basis of comparison slightly damped the romance of the reindeer but we replied firmly that we wanted to go by reindeer and asked if he would try if at all possible. He said he would be along at nine o'clock the next morning if conditions permitted. He didn't come; so, giving in, we phoned up the little plane.

We were faced with an awkward situation: the snow was melting so rapidly that it might become impossible either for the reindeer to travel or for the plane to land, whilst the road remained impassable. In that case we should have been stuck for a week or two. We were entering the supremely awkward season in Lapland, when for a time no plane can land except on a properly cleared airfield, the surface is too soft for the reindeer to go over it, the side roads are impassable to cars, the rivers are too nearly melted to be safe for overland transport but nowhere near being melted enough to take boats, and the disappearing snow gives a dampness to the atmosphere from which it is normally free.

However, the plane landed safely, we got in and in a few moments were over Inari, then dropping down and rushing straight towards the end of the lake. We couldn't possibly get down in time, I thought; but the little plane needed only an amazingly small landing space, and we walked safely back into the centre of Inari village.

Then I noticed how different it looked. One's perspective changes. When we were first considering living in Lapland, Ivalo seemed tiny. After a while Ivalo grew and became quite big, but Inari, with only 250 inhabitants, was still a little village. On returning from Menesjärvi, however, Inari had become a big busy place full of shops and houses and city life. One was back in town again, one felt.

13 : *Summer Midnight*

"Look, look!" cried Arja. "The ice is going down the river!"

The second spring had arrived. For some time the snow had been slowly disappearing; a week or two ago the busy pedestrian traffic across the river had suddenly died; and now, at last, the ice on the Ivalo River had broken up and was floating down to lose itself in Inari Lake. I ran outside: the inert white plain between us and the school had disappeared, and instead a sapphire torrent was rushing past, carrying with it a multitude of strangely shaped white pyramids. The river had come out of hibernation.

The ice swirled by, fierce and gay, like the broken decorations from a huge wedding cake. It continued for two or three days; sometimes there would be a lull, then as the thaw reached further and further up the river fresh masses would break loose and come swimming by. From time to time we heard the boom of explosions lower down; the ice held in it a latent aggressiveness and, if checked, would damn the river and flood the district. Where this started to happen men were at work blasting the ice free. Not so very long ago there had been severe floods in Ivalo in springtime: now the course of the river had been altered slightly and watch was kept to see that it flowed freely.

Even so, there was little to spare. Day after day the water rose higher and higher, coming across the stretch of grass below our house, then climbing up the steeper slope to the higher ground on which the house was built, and finally lapping round the path which led to our door. At last, when we had decided that if it came any nearer we ought to start carrying furniture upstairs, the waters slowly receded, leaving behind them a strange collection of treasure trove—odd bits of wood, part of a seat, a barrel of berries unfortunately too knocked about to be of any use.

Life quickened towards its summer pace—but not without hesitation. Many people suffered from "spring tiredness"—a well-known Lapland phenomenon—a lack of energy when the spring came after the exhausting winter. It was only a pause; in summer energy seemed boundless and—to many—sleep hardly necessary.

Lilian, who was now about a year and nine months old,

showed no surprise when the sun failed to set, nor had she expressed any criticism of the long nights of winter; but, like other children in Lapland, she showed no wish to go to bed until very late in the evening. How far should children be allowed to sleep and eat when they feel inclined and how far should they be habituated to an invariable timetable? In Lapland it was impossible to avoid a big swing in sleeping times between winter and summer; and, indeed, it seemed wrong to prevent a child from getting the maximum benefit whilst the sun was with us. Lilian, however, would one day return to the routine of the industrial world south of the Arctic Circle. It would be dangerous if in this malleable period she had become completely out of synchronism with it. So an artificial night was created—a dark blind pulled down when it was her bedtime. The sun was so strong that even then it burst through the barriers put up against it and by two o'clock in the morning the room was half light.

This worked to a limited extent; but a good deal of persuasion was usually necessary to induce her to go to bed.

"Pekka's in bed," we would say soothingly. "Maija's in bed, Sirkka-Liisa's in bed, all the children are going to sleep now."

"Then who's that shouting outside?" Lilian would ask cynically; and unfortunately, tiny tots in Lapland were sometimes still playing out at times when most English parents are asleep.

During that second summer there were several weeks of brilliant weather when the winter seemed like a forgotten dream. I wondered how much Lilian remembered of it. As she staggered happily through the tall grasses clutching armfuls of golden *kulleroita*—flowers like large buttercups, growing in profusion in the field next to us—did she ever think of the time when she was pushing her little red *kelkka* through the snow? When she splashed naked in the river, did she remember her winter clothing—layers and layers of it, trousers upon trousers, so much padding that she could fall down without hurting herself?

It was during this summer that we spent a good deal of time with Martti Mäenpää, the chief forester, and his wife Helvi. The first thing that marked Martti out from other men was that he lived in a house of stone; and that, in Ivalo, was very rare indeed, since almost all dwellings were wooden. It had belonged to a former chemist and later bought by the Forest Administration. Martti had his office downstairs and he and his family lived upstairs. He had three children: an older boy and girl who were at school, and little plump Malla, who was the same age as Lilian and who frequently exchanged baby gossip with her.

Martti was a tall man in his late thirties, with flowing bushy hair, a friendly smile, and a determined chin. He was not very talkative, but could give a great deal of information when he did. He occupied a unique position in Ivalo. He was responsible for the care of the forests in that area, which was beyond the line at which forestry was normally considered profitable. Before he came, only about two dozen men were employed on forestry work in that district; under his guidance the number had risen to several hundred and the Forest Administration had become the biggest employer of labour in the neighbourhood. He worked very long hours and for two or three years had cut out holidays altogether.

Martti once said to Arja that he had been walking through the forest when he first came to Ivalo, thinking over the problems of unemployment in the commune, and the feeling came to him then that this need not be so. If risks were run and roads constructed to the good timber, it could be taken out profitably and employment greatly increased. So, instead of just letting his job tick over, he spent days and nights working out the details of what could be done and then took the risks—with enormous benefit to Ivalo, and, incidentally, to the State of Finland, which received a considerable profit.

He possessed an expert knowledge of the geography of the commune, most of which had been photographed from the air, and in his company we made expeditions to places which we might otherwise never have known existed.

One evening Martti rang up and asked if we would like to go fishing. It was not early when we started—between eight and nine o'clock in the evening, after the children had gone to bed. We drove a few miles down the main Rovaniemi road, then turned off along a much smaller road not marked on the maps. Logs can be removed over the snow in winter, but for extensive cutting operations a permanent base is usually established which may remain for a number of years. Rough roads are constructed for communication with such a base; Martti himself had been responsible for some of them, and it was along one of these logging roads that we went. These logging roads can—in fact have to—take heavy lorries; they need to be negotiated with circumspection in a small car as there are liable to be damp and muddy stretches in which one may get stuck.

The road wound between the quiet hills, apparently abandoned; then, suddenly, we came on the logging camp—three big lorries were standing piled high with wood by the side of a long low wooden building, and nearby in the forest were machines for sawing up logs, and piles of sawdust. We wriggled through the logging camp and drove on through the forest until eventually we reached the Luttojoki, tumbling by the side of the road in the evening light. The Luttojoki starts as a tiny trickle near Kaunispää, not far from the main Rovaniemi road; a pretty little stream one can stride across easily.

Many other streams run into this tiny trickle, which broadens out until it becomes the lovely, slow-moving Luttojoki, the Lutto River. Increasing in size all the way the Luttojoki finally goes across the border and disappears into Russia. There it passes through Suonikylä, the area in which the Kolta Lapps formerly lived, and so into the Arctic Ocean. Fishing in it is for trout and salmon.

We unloaded the fishing gear; Martti and the driver of the car went to look at some nets they had left earlier whilst the rest of us gathered wood and made a fire. It was a wonderful place for fishing; in addition to the river on one side there was a lake on the other. You could take your choice. I tried in the lake, without, however, having any success. I am a friend to fish; I have very rarely succeeded in catching any. Martti was the most generous of men and sometimes pointed out where he knew fish to be, giving me the first chance of taking them.

Towards midnight the fire was burning comfortably; the others had secured a number of fish and three or four of these were cooking in front of the fire, impaled on stakes. There is an extraordinarily good taste about fish cooked, as soon as it has been caught, over a wood fire at midnight, and a queer magic about eating it in that strange luminosity of the Arctic summer night. Then one notices that the light is slowly increasing again and knows that the early hours of the morning have started. It is time to go home, though one is tempted to stay up all night.

On a second occasion we crossed the Luttojoki and penetrated into the forest on the far side. Martti had the use of a wooden hut and it was for this that we were making. We walked steadily through apparently trackless forest for several miles.

"How do you know the way?" I asked.

"Oh, we just follow the path," came the reply. To me there was no trace of anything remotely resembling a path.

The hut was on a small cleared slope leading down to a lake. Far away from the road, inaccessible by water, with no space for a plane to land, it was a place where a man might call his soul his own. It consisted of one room and a *sauna*; the room had a kind of wooden platform going round it, and at night we put blankets on this and slept there. It was a glorious summer night; some of the party went walking till the early hours of the morning, sleeping in the *sauna* on their return so as not to disturb the rest of us.

Lilian was by this time thought old enough to join these trips into the wilds, and both she and Malla had come with the party. Legs still not two years old had not lasted very long through the rough forest, however, and the two little girls had been carried a good part of the way there. I was not looking forward to the journey back. But rough carpentry is an ability which Lapland develops; Martti took an axe, a few odd pieces of wood that were lying around, and in a short while had knocked together a "wilderness chariot"—a kind of stretcher with two seats in it and handles fore and aft for carrying. Installed in this the two little ladies progressed regally back through the forest.

We saw an elk during the afternoon, its big horns showing for a second as it crossed a stream. Unlike reindeer, elk may be hunted, though a fair price is put on this. During the season elk meat is served as a somewhat expensive delicacy in the Lapland hotels. I failed to find any thrill in the idea of seeing one of these beautiful creatures dead.

This place was, we agreed, rather remote for those of us who had only learnt to walk a few months previously, and the next time we spent a week end in the wilds we went to a destination which could be reached by road—a disused logging hut. There was a road all the way to the hut, but it had degenerated so much at its farther end that we had to walk the last mile and a half.

The hut stood by a small lake, with the hills rising round it; though at first invisible, a channel led out of the lake and could be used for transporting logs. The hut consisted of one long main room with two-tier wooden bunks on either side, one small room and a kitchen. Here the forest workers lived, the married ones going home every week or fortnight. This they could easily do since there were roads and transport available in this district—and that undoubtedly had a profoundly beneficial effect.

There was little evidence left in the hut to show how the men spent their spare time; the only piece of evidence I found was a piece of cardboard roughly drawn out as a draught board. I asked Martti how much a forest worker would earn.

"Between twenty-five thousand and a hundred and fifty

thousand a month," he replied. This was in Finnmarks, at about nine hundred to the pound sterling, so this would be between twenty-three and a hundred and thirty-five pounds a month. "It depends on the man and the work," went on Martti. "A lorry driver makes about one thousand four hundred a day —on the average. Some make more. One man was once paid six million (i.e. about five thousand five hundred pounds) in a year for himself and his lorry. He had to maintain the lorry out of this—it wasn't all for himself."

Some of the forest workers must therefore have been earning a comparatively high income. It was difficult, in Ivalo, to know what a man's position really was: riding boots and an old jacket might have concealed either poverty or a fair amount of hard cash. Most days the men did not dress to impress. In the case of the Lapps, position could not be assessed purely in terms of money. A Lapp might have very little apparent income, yet own his own small house, have free fuel from the forests and fish in the rivers, and shoot a bird from time to time—his real standard of living would be much more comfortable than the figures lead one to believe.

Rough and primitive though life in the forest might be, there were certainly some who liked it. Many kinds of people found their way to Lapland; one never knew who might appear from the depths of the forest. Once a man came to see us who spoke quite good English; he had previously been some time in Canada.

"He's a good man, that Mäenpää," he said, referring to Martti, and then went on to talk about himself. "I like my work," he told me. "You can be independent in the forest. One day I work hard, if I want to, and then another day go off shooting."

Martti himself had a very high reputation in Ivalo, where he was looked upon as a public benefactor because of the employment he had created.

To return, however, to our own experiences in the hut in the forest, these were complicated by the fact that Lilian took a dislike to the hut and refused to go to sleep there. Nothing we said would persuade her; she demanded loudly to be taken back home, which was impossible that night. The situation was critical as there was both a series of children of assorted ages and some adults in the same room, and it looked as though a chain reaction might start. So we took her out, loaded her on to a two-wheeled cart which was standing outside, and I pushed her for a quarter of a mile over the rough bumpy road; after the first hundred yards she passed out and by the time we arrived back she was so sound asleep that she could be carried inside and put into her bunk. Unfortunately she later woke up and fell out of bed; in order to avoid disturbing the others we had to finish the night in the *sauna*.

The night—and "night" at that time of the year meant simply a moderation of the daylight and nothing approaching darkness—was so magical that sleep seemed almost a crime anyway. A friend back in Ivalo laughed when we told him of Lilian's reactions. "She's like an old forest worker," he said. "Insists on sleeping outside." One or two of the older people, who remember the days when the forest workers slept outside —in winter in two lines with a fire blazing between them— consider that life nowadays is getting too soft.

After this experience we decided that we ought to have our own summer hut, or *kämppä*. Throughout Finland everyone who possibly can has some kind of summer hide-out, usually a small wooden building, large enough to sleep in and with a *sauna*, by the side of some quiet lake or river. This was equally true in Lapland, the people who lived in Ivalo regarding it as an urban area from which one sought to escape to fresh air and peace. The summer huts in Lapland—like other Lappish dwellings—were even farther away and more isolated than those of southern Finland. During the summer months it was usually difficult to get hold of anyone since most people disappeared to their refuge on all possible occasions.

We thought, however, that this was rather too big a proposition for us to undertake by ourselves—since we did not intend to stay in Lapland for ever—so we formed an association with Martti and Gunnar, who also had young families. It was, from our point of view, a most profitable partnership, since Gunnar was the owner of the Ivalo saw mill and Martti controlled logging operations as well as knowing the possible sites and having the power to rent them out. A site for such a summer hut may be owned—freehold—or it may be rented from the Forest Administration at a low rental. We settled on a site not far from the road which ran from Ivalo towards the east—we did not fancy having to carry Lilian very many miles. There had been a Lappish house and farm there, but it was disused and nobody seemed to want it. There was, of course, a lake; and since nobody else came there it felt virtually like our private stretch of water. The hut was very quickly ready under Martti's direction: one room, with a brick fireplace and a wood cooker, and one other tiny room at one end.

We spent many week ends there that summer, usually going in the early morning and returning in the late evening:

sometimes fishing in the lake, sometimes walking, and some-times merely clearing up the surroundings. We kept it up to the verge of winter; and my latest memory is of coming back from a walk through the falling snow, hurrying towards the cheerful, shining light in the hut and the rest of the party snugly playing cards inside.

It was, perhaps, best in autumn, when the berries were ripening and could be gathered. Black, red, and yellow, they spread out under the dwarf birches and amidst the brown and yellow fungi and the soft light mosses: the greeny-orange bear moss and the *seinäsammal* or wall moss. This was formerly used for jamming between the wood of which houses were built to make them draught-free. Nowadays modern manu-factured insulating materials have taken its place.

Yet sometimes I had doubts about the hut. Was it not con-tradictory to spend most of one's time working hard so that in the leisure hours one could afford to go and live in the way one might have lived before modern civilization existed? And, if the desire for this sort of life really were a part of our nature, did it make sense for our Western society to spend so much of its energy trying to eliminate just this contact with the primitive?

I also felt sometimes another latent desire—to live alone, with my family, very simply, in a really remote place; to spend the day finding and cooking food and gathering wood for fuel; but to be in an environment which one understood, and where the results of work were simple and direct. It occurred to me that our intensive search for knowledge had resulted in a situation in which we were surrounded with devices about which we knew very little. These feelings are not unknown in Lapland; I was told that many who lived for long periods there did get the urge to move further and further out—from Ivalo to Inari, from Inari into the wilds.

Even the more technical side of life in Ivalo, however, could sometimes have a charm and pleasant humanity in summer. One day Tauno Nykänen, the head of the electricity under-taking, kindly invited me to go out with them on a trip they were making to a new school and to look at something which had gone wrong with a transformer somewhere beyond Inari.

Nykänen was a sturdily built man a few years older than I was. He was proud that although theoretically he only held the qualification of "technician", he was doing work frequently carried out by an "engineer". The titles "technician", "en-gineer" and "diploma engineer" have a very exact meaning in

Finland, each corresponding to a certain standard of training. He had the right, in my opinion, to his pride, since the service was very good, and, despite the severe climate, very rarely interrupted.

I had first heard something of him the year before, when there had been a general strike which had almost brought Finland to a standstill for three weeks. In Ivalo, with no postal services operating, we had been virtually cut off from the world during this time; but the feelings there had been milder, and the strikers reluctant to take action against people they knew personally. They had, however, threatened to stop work at the power station, and Nykänen had remarked: "In that case I shall go up and run it myself."

This was quite possible, since the power station itself was not large. It was a square white building about five or ten miles north of Ivalo along the Inari road. Three spherical lamps burned continuously in front of it and at the back a pipe made of wooden boards held together by metal bands ran up to a lock gate fourteen metres higher. Inside a turbine sat like a big green pig with its nose to the place where the water came in. Another generating set was going to be installed but at that time had not arrived. Overhead wires on wooden poles went up to Inari and down to Ivalo, reaching their farthest limit at the airfield seven miles south of Ivalo. One of the biggest loads was the saw mill in Ivalo, and if a heavy load came on this the lights throughout the district went down.

I climbed into the cab of the lorry belonging to the electricity undertaking this fine morning at the end of the summer and we set off towards Inari. After an hour watching patterns of lake and forest colour going past we reached Inari and went for coffee at the house of one of the men working in the organization. Our destination was a school off the main road; the lorry was loaded up with a drum of cable, spades and other working tools, sugar and food for the school.

Over the coffee we discussed the equipment they were using. Cable was made at the Finnish cable works; insulators came from the "Arabia" factory in Helsinki, one of the largest potteries in Europe; the other items were without exception made in Finland. It showed how independent Finland can be, even in engineering: no easy export market here.

There was no through road to the school, so we dropped the cable and other supplies by the side of a lake, to be brought by motor boat, then turned and drove up a side road along which the vehicle lurched and swayed like a ship in a rough sea. Below in the valley ran the power line going to the saw which had the faulty transformer. We bumped round a bend and drew up where it was operating.

After being cut down the tree trunks had been left floating in the lake. They made grey and silver patches in the sunshine, with a thin log boundary holding them together. Some distance from this was the end product, piles of planks waiting to be taken away; and in between the saw was working. A conveyor belt with iron teeth ran down to the water; the logs were placed on this and hauled up, then pushed across to the saw. This consisted of five gigantic hacksaw blades jigging up and down. The wood was gripped at one end and supported in the middle on a carriage; the saw screamed hysterically as the log went through, and five planks were held and removed by another carriage on the far side. Another machine smoothed the edges of the planks. The whole was outside in the fresh air.

The faulty transformer was in a metal box about a couple of feet high; Tauno Nykänen opened it up and found a wire which had come loose. He repaired this. Our party was now four strong: Nykänen, myself, the driver, and another man who had arrived on a big red motor cycle.

The last two were carrying guns. They nodded to their chief, said, "See you later," and disappeared into the woods. Nykänen and I set out along the path. "They say this is a motor road," he said, looking at the trail which wandered through trees and marshes, liberally sprayed with potholes. "Hm." His tone indicated that he would not have put any motor vehicle on that road, and neither should I. But it was the sort of morning when one could welcome the fact of having to walk. Apparently caught by the same spirit as the two who had gone off, the chief put a piece of stick over his shoulder like a gun and stuck his document case on the end of it.

We had to go along one of the old post paths. For part of its distance this was made of logs thrown over a swamp which glowed green and gold underneath the ancient grey trunks. Presently we came over a ridge and saw a half-built school in front of us; below the path sloped down to some farm buildings with behind them a red wooden home for orphans. The motor boat was coming across the lake; it pulled up at a landing stage and a tractor rushed to meet it, driving exuberantly straight into the water, over a large boulder and up to the side of the boat.

After we had had some more coffee Nykänen examined the layout of the new cable to the school. Half-way through the afternoon the other two arrived and put their guns in a box at the bottom of the pole holding a transformer. They hadn't managed to shoot anything. We then went round opening doors, looking in everywhere, standing back meditatively and generally preparing the way for an electrical installation.

We returned home in the evening through the brilliant hues of autumn; it was September, and already the evenings were getting short.

The school we had visited was at Riutula; this is on another route out of Inari, a route which is still mostly a path, and along which the post goes until it reaches the border at Angeli —in winter by reindeer. The school was part of an orphanage, perhaps the most northerly orphanage in the world. Faced with the task of complete rebuilding though it had been since the war, the commune had not neglected to make provision for its lonely children; and soon they would possess a new and modern school.

14: *Nellim and the Bay of Gold*

PAST our house the road ran to the east. It was in one way a mysterious road, for it had no proper destination and no end: it went to the Russian border thirty miles away and there, for most people, it stopped.

Before the war this road had run through Finnish territory up the eastern side of Lake Inari to Petsamo and the Arctic Ocean. It had been the main outlet to the north, and Nellim, a village about five miles this side of the border, had then been far bigger. The peace treaty at the end of the war removed this outlet to the ocean from Finland entirely, making it Russian-controlled territory; the new border sliced off the road just beyond Nellim. The traffic to the north swung across to the other route through Inari and into Norway. This route was developed rapidly.

This placing of the border had one other effect. It took from Finland and gave to Russia useful rapids north-east of Nellim, rapids which could supply considerable hydro-electric power. The U.S.S.R. immediately started to develop these, but in a rather special way. They gave the work of building power stations to the Finns, to the Imatra Power Company, in which the Finnish State holds a controlling interest. The Imatra Power Company was responsible for the design and construction of the stations, for which it received an agreed fee.

One of these stations—at Jäniskoski—had been built before we arrived in Lapland, and the second, at Rajakoski, was completed during the first year we were there. A third was planned. The output of the Rajakoski station was 41,000 kilowatts, or over forty times that of the installation which supplied the whole of Inari commune. There was no doubt, therefore, that the territory on the other side of the border was being developed rapidly.

On our side of the border, however, was a wonderfully lonely and untouched stretch of country on the eastern side of Lake Inari. In the heart of this lived an interesting character—Paavo Pandy. There were, at that time, very few residents of non-Finnish descent in Inari commune. One was myself, the latest arrival; another was a woman known as "Moppe-Rouva", reputed to have been extremely beautiful in her younger days and to have an Italian ancestry; and a third was Paavo Pandy. Pandy's father came from an aristocratic Hungarian family; his mother was a Finn. He had lived, earlier, at Virtaniemi; but some time between 1930 and 1940 he had moved out to a very isolated spot with a romantic name—Kultalahti, the "Bay of Gold". Here he lived with his family by fishing, hunting, growing vegetables, and owning reindeer.

In the late summer of the second year we went to visit Pandy. We travelled to Nellim by bus; the road wound between lonely hills with here and there an isolated house or sign pointing to a footpath. Four miles from Ivalo there was a small lake, Akujärvi, with a village and school; a side road here led to the Luttojoki River and eventually finished up at the border, further south. A few miles further on another road led off to a hut formerly used by forest workers but now available in spring for ski-ers, and owned by the commune.

Past this point the road wound and twisted over gentle hills; on either side was the forest, but sometimes the trees were only blackened trunks. This was "burnt Lapland", which had suffered so much during the war. At last the road reached Nellim; a few wooden houses, a school and a shop clustered round a long finger of water from Lake Inari. The children at this school were less sophisticated than those in Ivalo.

Sometimes they would return late to school after a holiday; late not by a few minutes or even hours, but by anything up to a week. They had been too busy with other affairs, they said. They had—sometimes—quite genuinely been helping with the work of the family—such as the reindeer round-up.

Some of the children from remote areas were, however, very conscientious. One girl came late to school and apologized to the teacher. "We had to ski sixty kilometres," she said, "and my little brother wouldn't go more than forty." She obviously regarded her little brother as a disgrace to the family. He was aged seven, and forty kilometres is twenty-five miles.

Those with any ability to paint at all find it greatly stimulated in Lapland. Many people try, some achieving only moderate results, some with real distinction; and they are joined by many others who come to Lapland to paint for their holidays. It is also the custom for artists to seek out likely customers and call with a selection of their paintings.

One of the teachers at the Nellim school, Sylvi Ahlquist, was an artist. We purchased two pictures from her; one of them seemed to convey the spirit of the flaring autumn, and the other, with its tones of blue and bare trees standing starkly in the foreground, suggested the mystery and tragedy and hope in this particular part of Lapland. Having looked at them nearly every day since then I still like them; and daily contact is a stern test of any affection.

Typical of Lapland, and seen in these pictures, is the *kelo-honka*, the tree which no longer lives, which perhaps has not been alive for many years, from which all leaves are gone, and yet which still stands erect and pointing to the sky, the colour of light smooth ash. In southern Finland such trees would be taken away; in Lapland they remain, dignified and untouched, in peaceful death.

South of the road footpaths led to isolated Lapp houses; there were some fifteen Kolta Lapps in the school. It was not possible to go far north on the eastern side of Lake Inari by walking without having to traverse the border region; this was illegal without the appropriate pass. By water, however, one could go all the way up Lake Inari. On one day a week this could be done by the post motor boat, which set off on Monday and came back about Thursday; otherwise it was necessary to find some boatman willing to make the trip.

We found one and set off with the boatman, his dog, a woman and a small boy in tartan overall and striped woollen cap who lost interest half-way through the trip and went to sleep under a raincoat. We travelled for an hour and a half between the scattered islands along the eastern edge of Inari; occasionally there would be a gap in the line of the shore and one would stare up some long inlet the end of which was lost in a misty line of trees. The islands moved to and fro in front of one another like green veils as the boat went past them. Finally we slid behind one of the islands and pulled up at a landing stage in a quiet channel. On one side a few white goats were grazing peacefully; on the other a house and farm buildings stood in a small clearing. Round the clearing ran a wooden fence, and behind the fence stretched the infinite forest. The trees seemed to be waiting quietly behind the wooden barrier for the first moment when vigilance should be relaxed and they could return.

The little boy gently woke up; the dog, which had been standing on the end of the boat, was greeted by another dog which rushed down to the shore, barking frenziedly at seeing one of its own kind. It, too, was native to the country; it belonged to a medium-sized sturdy breed which can be trained either as a hunting dog or as a "sheepdog" for reindeer. A comfortable-looking woman followed. Round her ran two rosy-cheeked boys, full of high spirits and showing no signs of being adversely affected by their remote northern situation; and

Races on the frozen Ivalo River

Reindeer skins hung outside for weathering during the winter

Girls in Lappish clothing reading journals, Ivalo School

Class in the continuation school, Ivalo

finally a tallish, fresh-faced man in his early fifties, Paavo Pandy himself.

Pandy had a flair for languages: he spoke English, French, German and Swedish in addition to Finnish and Hungarian, and he had plenty of ideas in any of them. During the war years when he had been in the army a good deal of his property had been destroyed, though fortunately not his house. He started again. He had been given some seeds by one of the relief organizations; with these, and what he had selected himself later on, he had built up a flourishing vegetable garden. At an exhibition in Rovaniemi he had once shown over fifty different varieties.

Presently he took us for a walk round his property. The house was at one end; at the back was a raised platform with spikes on which hay was stored; a long building in which the goats lived in winter, and another dark wooden building; a hut, supported above the ground to protect it from animals; a well in the centre; and at the other end was the vegetable garden. We walked through this to a large smoking metal cylinder; inside, on a wire mesh near the top, were the bones of some animal, and below some slowly burning fragrant branches. This, Pandy explained, was goat meat: it was being smoked over juniper branches, and we were to have some for supper. My eyes had opened wide at the long lines of vegetables, the potatoes and the carrots, the spinach and the parsley, the beans and peas, and the lettuce, all growing abundantly. Later we sat down to supper. The goat meat was excellent: Pandy's wife was a good cook; Pandy said he had taught her his Hungarian recipes. There was, however, about the vegetables, something more even than good cooking alone could produce. The taste, whether it was due to careful selection of the seeds, to the soil, or to the unceasing sun of the Arctic summer, was remarkable.

It was, therefore, in summer quite possible to grow ample vegetables as far north as this, but the growing season was very short. As soon as the snow was gone they had to be in the ground, which ought to have been dug over before it froze. The ground softened in May or June, and by the end of August the cultivator had to start protecting them against chance frosts. That same evening we saw Pandy up at the end of the vegetable rows lighting a fire.

Later I myself did some experiments with growing lettuce; it came up red.

Pandy's house had a big living-kitchen, with two rooms opening off it which could be used as bed-sitting-rooms, and one or two other odd rooms and lofts. A flap opened up in the middle of the living-kitchen to reveal the cellar. Pandy had, therefore, a certain amount of accommodation for letting to travellers which was, for its remoteness, very comfortable. At the time we were there the other bed-sitting-room was occupied by two Hungarians, of the very few who had been allowed to travel abroad that year. Pandy considerately spoke English with me, Finnish with my wife, and Hungarian with the Hungarians. It didn't end there, however. With Arja and the Hungarian woman he spoke German, since this was the best language they had in common; but with Arja and the Hungarian man he spoke Swedish.

Pandy's windows had a Hungarian air about them: on the outside they could be completely closed by two solid wooden flaps. These were painted red on the outside and had a heart cut out of the middle. His toilet (which of course was outside, well away from the house and not far from where the goats lived in winter) also had its own atmosphere. It was spacious and decorated inside with coloured pictures from the periodicals of various nations. Arja asserts that these included portraits of British Royalty.

Then I walked into something bigger than I expected. I got lost. I had thought once or twice that it would be an interesting experience to be lost in Lapland; but always, of course, with proper preparation, good equipment, and suitable maps. Unfortunately one doesn't usually get lost when one is expecting it. I went astray when I had gone out for half an hour's walk before lunch, with only light clothing, no maps, and— worst of all—no knife. Every man going away from the town in Lapland carries a Finnish or Lappish knife in his belt, a short knife which can be used for slicing meat, cutting wood, or for killing an animal. Normally I did the same—but why should one need a knife when going for half an hour's walk before lunch? Arja had already returned to Ivalo; I was staying a day or two longer, and about eleven o'clock I thought I would look for a waterfall to which Pandy had taken the whole party the previous day. I found it in fifteen minutes or so: a poetical little dell with a tiny water splash cascading down the rock at one end. I started back in what I thought was the correct direction; it should have led past a marsh.

I came to a marsh, skirted round it, and took what I thought was the right path. I went along it some way. It ended abruptly.

Perhaps I had been going too much to one side: the proper path, however, could not be far off. I walked across a log which looked as though it had been placed by design across a swamp.

It led to another track which went a little way into the forest and again ended abruptly.

I left that and tried another. I tried many times. The forest semed full of paths—determined paths which suddenly ended up at a tree; inviting paths which ran pleasantly downwards and left me looking at a heap of stones; convincing paths which lost their confidence and petered out to nothingness in the middle of the wilderness. At last I saw the truth. The paths were simply misleading. They were tracks made by reindeer in pursuit of their own ends and were of no help at all. They went nowhere.

I realized, also, that I had been going for two hours and the walk back should not have taken more than twenty minutes.

I decided to abandon the paths and trust to my sense of direction; overconfident, perhaps, but I had not grasped how lost I was. Every moment I expected to see the fence round Pandy's place. I continued expecting to see it till about three o'clock in the afternoon; the situation was still a joke; I had missed my lunch, that was all. I walked for some time up gentle hills with no characteristic landmarks, over rocks between the thousands of trees which watched me silently and unhelpfully. I went across green-covered, oozing swamps.

It was all familiar. This was exactly what we had seen the previous day when we were only a few yards from home. It was so familiar that I felt constantly reassured; I could not be far from that fence and Kultalahti.

Then suddenly a horrible suspicion hit me. I was crossing a swamp with a log and a stone in it. All perfectly natural—but surely the last swamp also had a log and a stone? And the one before as well? Could it possibly be the same log and the same stone and the same swamp?

I had read tales of travellers who got lost and wandered round in circles and had thought: "This couldn't happen to me. I should never be so stupid. I should know." I now realized that inside a Lappish forest, unless you are born and bred there and feel the landmarks in your blood, you haven't any sense of direction at all. You cannot see round or through or over the trees; they stretch away, boundlessly, in each direction; and each direction looks the same.

I decided to abandon any attempt to find the house and instead make for Lake Inari. Following the shore must then eventually take me home, however long the journey. I found a fairly high hill and saw through the trees a flash of water; it was much farther away than it should have been. As soon as I left the top of the hill I lost sight of the water, and when next I could see the lake I was even farther from it.

I was now taking the situation seriously. I realized that the next house—if there were a next house—might be twenty miles away, and that behind—in whichever direction that might be—stretched uninhabited forest broken only by the border with Russia, five or six miles away. I didn't want to wander over that. Up to that time, also, I had felt that being lost was a very interesting experience. It now occurred to me that one could get lost and stay lost.

Electronic engineers have to study many subjects which seem of little direct use to them, such as hydraulics and theory of structures. When the need for these had been queried, the answer had always been given: "Yes, but your education must have a broad basis. What if you were to change the direction of your career?" I had done that, and now wondered which of these subjects was going to get me out of a forest in north-east Lapland. I decided, however, that one thing I could do: I could manage to go in a straight line. In this way I should get somewhere sooner or later, even if it was the Arctic Ocean.

What I could do was to beam myself from tree to tree: start from tree one where I was standing, go to tree two not too far ahead, and from tree two choose tree three in line with trees one and two, advancing from tree to tree in this way. Then a better idea struck me. There was no sun, or direction finding would have been easy; the sky was overclouded; but how about the wind? It had a cool, damp feel as though it might be coming from the water. I thought I would take a chance on it.

The guess about the wind was right; I walked straight against the breeze and after some time came out on the shore of the lake. It looked very beautiful and very strange; Kultalahti, where Pandy lived, should however be somewhere on my right. If I rounded a short projection I ought to be there.

After five minutes' walking I could see the bay fully—very like the required one but with no fence, no buildings, not a sign of human life on it. I went on; perhaps it was the next one. Another beautiful curving shore came into sight, very much like Kultalahti, but—quite empty. Nothing but forest and water and rocks.

This is the second degree of being lost—when having realized that you are lost, and having worked out what to do, and come again to what you think is familiar ground, and turned the corner beyond which you have calculated lies home —you find it isn't there. There was nothing to do but keep walking. Some time I must reach Kultalahti.

I had now been in the forest, entirely out of contact with my own species, for several hours; and two quite novel feelings were see-sawing up and down inside me. The first was a growing sense of amazement that man, this frail complicated creature with no more to help him than I had got, had ever managed to survive. How had he done it? How had he managed to get food and to keep himself alive in the early days? My respect for the intelligence of primitive man was going up. But coupled with this was the realization that we were not cut off from nature; we were a part of it. And nature was on our side.

It was a strange realization, for although I love nature, I am no sentimentalist about it. Nature, with its pattern of life preying endlessly on life, is at times so cruel that it cannot be contemplated without a shudder. Previously, I had regarded nature half as an enemy and thought that without that complex apparatus for providing houses and food and clothing which is our society—I should be lost. Now I had suddenly become aware that the same force, whatever it might be, which had produced man and kept him in existence was still operating. Take away all my civilized background and there was still something left —a latent power to call forth previously unknown abilities to meet the situation.

It was a far-reaching realization, going much beyond my immediate situation. It meant that man's immediate fate was no longer so disturbing. Even if all he had made should be destroyed, he would find the ability to start anew; even if he should obliterate himself there was still that latent creativity working. The story would not be ended.

But coupled with this reassuring realization was another one with a touch of panic in it. I had no evidence at all except my own memory that any other human being existed. There was no trace of man's work, no sign in the forest or the lake or the sky that any human hand had ever been there. The paths might all have been made by reindeer, and quite probably were. A queer voice inside me was saying: "What if you should never again meet a human being?"

I answered it: "Of course I shall soon meet human beings again. I have only to look long enough and I shall find them."

But the voice went on: "Until you do find them you cannot be certain that there are any other human beings. You have no real evidence that they exist. Perhaps you are the only creature of your sort in an endless forest."

Of course it was a foolish voice, and I did not propose to pay much attention to it, but I wished—oh how I wished—that I could meet someone. *Anyone.* I have frequently wanted to escape into solitude and cursed the crowded cities, but at that moment human society appeared extremely desirable. I do not know who my worst enemy is, but if he had come along I should have greeted him with a shout of joy and offered to pick him some berries.

Then, lying on the path, I saw a cigarette packet. Normally I detest litter, but, under those circumstances the cigarette packet, even empty, seemed a beautiful thing. Someone must have gone along this path. Perhaps I was not far from Kulta-lahti or if not that, some other dwelling. I hurried along until I had been going along the lakeside for an hour and a half.

There wasn't a sign of anything I had ever seen before. The cigarette packet was deceptive, perhaps dropped there a long time ago. (I learned later that there was a house in this direction, many miles away, but that it was uninhabited.)

I sat down for a long think. There were some berries near me; I ate them, reflecting that it might be a long time before I got any other food. The only solution to the problem that I could see was that I had got so mixed up that I had come out on the other side of Kultalahti—so that it was on my left and not my right. This did not seem possible, but was the only answer I could think of unless the whole landscape had been changed by some supernatural agency. I turned, and after another hour and a half was back at the point where I had come out on to the lake.

Suddenly there were three distant shots. They sounded in the right direction; a hope sprang up that they might be a signal. With a new spring in my step I pressed forward. I had still some way to go, but I followed the edge of the lake meticu-lously without making any short cuts through the forest. At last I rounded the final corner; there, more wonderful than I could ever have believed them a day ago, were the coloured wooden buildings of Pandy's establishment.

The time was eight o'clock and they had been looking for me for some time and fired four groups of three shots.

"We've kept your lunch," said Pandy. No other establish-ment has ever saved a meal for me quite as long as this. Eight o'clock in the evening is a late lunch time, but I soon finished the food before me, ample though it was. During the time I had been walking I had not felt particularly hungry, but when an hour later they offered me my dinner, I ate that as well.

Later over a map I tried to work out where I had been. My trail did not even seem to have gone in circles; it looked more like a lover's knot. One way, said Pandy, to find your direction was to follow the water; it all ran down into Lake Inari. I should not, however, have been able to wander unknowingly over the border; a reindeer fence has been built round the whole northern boundary of Finland, and to cross the border one would have to climb this. It is very easy to get lost in Lapland; a hundred yards into the forest from the road, and you don't know in which direction it is.

To go away from Lapland, or to come back to it, gave me a sense of shock—it was like going through the looking glass. The time when that sense of shock was even greater, however, was on returning from the short stay with Pandy. It seemed that there was less difference between London and Ivalo than between Ivalo and the depths of Lapland. For once I had been right off the highway and into the wilderness; the effect remained, and at times the forest seemed still around me. At night I would feel to be tossing in a soft green bed with strange dreams haunting me. It was some time before I could lose these impressions and get down to seeing that the heating system was in order for the winter.

15: A Winter's Tale

THERE was much more than the coming winter to be thought about. In December we expected our second child. It would have been possible to have this in the hospital in Ivalo; but as the birth was not likely to be straightforward and as Arja's mother was in Helsinki she decided to go there.

For the period during which she would not be working in Ivalo it was necessary to find a substitute. Arja complained that the law allowed a doctor to take a final-year student as substitute, but in the case of a dentist only a fully qualified person was permissible, and it was not easy to persuade these to come to Lapland. Eventually, however, she came to an agreement with a young woman called Ilona Kaukoranta-Ilveskivi.

Ilona was a pretty girl from a professional Helsinki family. She was a good photographer; fond of music; and spoke English which she had learned mainly by her own efforts. What marked her out, however, was her great liking for Lapland and also the fact that she was married to a man whose work was the most typical of Lapland. Heikki, her husband, dark-haired and with a humorous face which had a touch of devilment in it, was a reindeer owner. After qualifying she had come to Sodankylä, a hundred miles south of Ivalo, and for some time we had known her as "the Sodankylä dentist". It was here she had met Heikki; at the time she came to Ivalo they had been married for some time and had one child.

We had already met Heikki; indeed he had given me my first ride behind a reindeer. That had been the previous spring; we had driven out with some friends to a reindeer round-up south of Ivalo. We had gone by car some twenty or thirty miles down the road, then left the vehicle and walked along a rough track which ran into the forest. The round-up had been going for some days when we got there. In one corner the skins of the slaughtered reindeer were hung up; a brightly coloured figure was walking along the road somewhat unsteadily as we approached. It had evidently been a satisfactory round-up.

We watched a few of the remaining reindeer being driven into the central enclosure and sorted out, then started back along the uneven track. Suddenly a reindeer pulling a man behind it stopped and the man called out to us. I did not recognize him at first, then after a moment I saw who it was—Heikki.

He was in Lappish clothing; previously I had only seen him in
a suit. He offered to give us a ride behind his reindeer, in turns.

There are two forms of sledge commonly pulled by reindeer
—the *kelkka* and the *pulkka*. Of these the *pulkka* is the smaller
one, chiefly used for fast personal transport. It is like a small
canoe, with room for little more than one person in it. Heikki
let the women and children of our party ride in the *pulkka*,
sitting behind and driving it himself. Then he asked if I
would like to have a go—alone. I said that I would; in my
mind there were certain reservations which I did not mention.
He handed me the reins and I sank into the *pulkka*.

The instant I was down the reindeer started off, and with a
wild swerving motion we slid along the track. The *pulkka*
seemed exceedingly ready to precipitate its occupant into the
snow, and the steadiness of the motion was not helped by the
fact that there were huge ruts in the road. The *pulkka* is so
small that one can barely put one's legs inside it and one is
tempted to keep them out to improve the uncertain balance.

Suddenly the reindeer saw a minor path to the right, swung
round and headed for the depths of the forest, easily leaving
the rest of the party behind. Heikki hurried across to try to cut
us off, but it looked as though he would be too late. I had no
idea as to how one controlled a reindeer, so I pulled on the
only thing available, and shouted loudly at it. One of these two
deterrents was effective and when the rest of the party came
running up breathlessly they found me sitting on the ground
grasping the rein firmly whilst the reindeer stared down at me
with those big innocent-looking eyes it has.

Ilona came to Ivalo to our house in the late autumn. Heikki,
who had to look after his reindeer, stayed in Sodankylä. There
were other new arrivals in Ivalo that year too. One of these was
a young man called Pentti Mäenpää (not to be confused with
the Chief Forester, Martti Mäenpää). Pentti had for some time
been living in Vuotso. In the Lapland way we had spoken of
him as "Vuotson Pentti"—Pentti from Vuotso. Vuotso was a
village between Ivalo and Sodankylä; it had simple accommodation for travellers but very little else. Pentti said that Vuotso
had been too quiet; he had come to Ivalo for the social life that
we had there.

Pentti was a fair-haired genial giant. He taught in the continuation school—the additional school attended by all those
who had only had primary education—in Ivalo. He also painted
pictures, collected gramophone records, made tables and sheds,
read a great deal, and owned reindeer. There were very few
sides of life which Pentti did not touch. We never knew in

what guise he would appear: he might arrive very smooth and smart in his best suit, or turn up in leggings and lumber-jacket with a coil of rope round his middle, straight from lassooing reindeer.

There were, according to Pentti, all sorts of ins and outs to this business of owning reindeer, and not least was the matter of personal relations.

"There was one schoolteacher," he said, "who bought thirty reindeer. He must have thought he was on better terms with the reindeer men than he really was." Pentti laughed. "Next year there wasn't one left. They told him the wolves had got them all."

In Lapland personal property is rarely taken, and there is little personal violence, but reindeer are on a different footing. Reindeer do sometimes end up with the wrong owner's marks on them, and in the case of a quarrel it is quite probable that revenge would be taken through a man's reindeer.

Pentti said that he did not often drink wine, since he had a weak stomach which would not stand it; he had to limit himself to whisky.

Another arrival in Ivalo was Annikki Setälä, an authoress who had published many stories with a Lapland setting. She lived in a house at the other end of Ivalo, the walls rich with books and pictures. She knew many aspects of Lapland life; she had travelled widely, in many countries, but it was here in Lapland peace that she had chosen to settle.

Both Annikki and Pentti spoke English and entered into the activities of the English Club, which was now reaching its peak. It had a much bigger membership in relation to the popula-tion than any of the English Clubs in the south, and in this its second year it had attracted a number of new members who were starting to learn English. It had even caught the attention of the Communists who, I was told, had begun to wonder what was going on. One of the local Communist leaders and his wife joined for a time.

There is a strong Communist movement in Finnish Lapland. Communists are, in fact, in the majority there. The deputy chairman of the council in Ivalo was a Communist. Communist propaganda was very marked during the elections: the Com-munists put up clear, attractively illustrated posters, which caught the eye immediately. None of the other parties had any-thing nearly as effective. It was also said that the Communists had two full-time organizers in Lapland.

It is not easy to be certain of the character of Finnish Com-munism. "Our Communists are not like other Communists," some Finns say. "They fought with the others in the war; they believe in friendship with Russia, but the independence of Finland." Without being inside the party, it is difficult to know.

Those English Club members who had started the previous year had by this time worked themselves up to the point of presenting a five-minute play.

There was a rather curious development of this short sketch. It was supposed to represent an English morning scene. Later the continuation school also acted this on the stage in the school hall. I had not imagined when I wrote the sketch that it was great drama, but I had supposed that it was thoroughly and incontrovertably English. But when those children, many of whom were Lappish, gave their version, this was not so. It was difficult to say what had happened; the words were all the same and very well pronounced, but the effect was indubitably Lappish. The pianist startled everyone at the end by suddenly and unexpectedly playing "God Save the Queen".

In November, however, we had left Ivalo for a time and were in Helsinki, which seemed much warmer and milder than it had done in the earlier years. Immediately outside Arja's mother's flat in Runeberginkatu was a taxi station: a terrible threat to the purse but very comforting to have there in any emergency. At half past two on the morning of 4th December we drove to Naistenklinikka; wreaths and veils of mist weaving round it gave the building an air of mystery which that dead hour of the night enhanced.

Our son was born in the morning, after an operation; and we decided to call him George Henry Aslak. A child with his roots in two countries has to have at least one name which can be pronounced in both; in this case the name was Henry. (A Finn putting down the sound of this name would write "Henri"—so that at times he has a Gallic air.) "Aslak" is a Lappish name; we were proud of his association with Lapland and thought he deserved this.

Arja considered the standard of maternity treatment which it was possible to get in Helsinki to be very high; and not only in Helsinki, but in most large centres. Almost all the women wanted to have their babies in hospital, but in remote places in Lapland things were difficult. There was, for example, the case of the woman from Lisma. Lisma was, even for Inari commune, remote. It was almost mid-way between the Rovaniemi–Ivalo road on the east and the Rovaniemi–Kilpisjärvi road on the west; about as deep into the wilderness as one could get, and not easily reached by water. This woman in Lisma was due to have a baby and she started out to go to Inari, where she could have it at the health centre under the care of the Inari midwife.

She first of all walked forty kilometres along forest paths to Menesjärvi. She had left it too late, however; at Menesjärvi she had to stop and the baby was born there, in a *sauna*. Mother and child were taken by car to Inari along the rough Menesjäriv–Inari road; after three days in the health centre at Inari the woman wanted to be up and starting on the walk back, carrying her child.

Life in "back" Lapland, even in places as remote as this, partly attracted me. I imagine that with a few changes in my make-up I could have taken to it. But I should have felt differently if I had been a woman. Amongst the professional families we knew it was usually the man who was in love with Lapland; the woman, less concerned with hunting and fishing in the open, more tied to looking after children in the home and providing meals in a district where prices were high, sometimes turned longing eyes towards the south. The woman, too, often suffered when the man was in an official position: during the ski-ing season and throughout the summer a succession of "official" visitors would have to be fed, housed, and entertained. She was worn out before the winter had even started.

Not all women felt the same: some liked even the most primitive Lapland life.

We returned to Ivalo in January. It was, fortunately, a much shorter and easier journey than my first one: Aero, the Finnish airline, were now running planes right up to Ivalo three times a week throughout the winter. Straight lines of blue and orange lights marked the gap in the forest where the plane came down to land; they shone brilliantly in the darkness, more brilliantly than those in Helsinki, sharper and clearer than those in London or Stockholm or any other place at which I had landed during the dark. This brilliance was no illusion but an unmistakable fact, produced by the extraordinarily dry and uncompromisingly pure atmosphere. My colour photographs taken in Lapland were at first always over-exposed; it was only after I had understood the translucence of the atmosphere that they improved; and then, when I came back from the north, I was wrong again—I gave too little exposure for the thicker atmospheres south of the Arctic Circle.

We returned to Ivalo: to the peace of Lapland, but not to any peaceful time in our lives. During her life in Lapland Lilian had hardly ever had a cold, had never had a serious illness, and had been glowingly healthy apart from one thing.

Dry, red, irritating patches would appear on her skin, sometimes small in extent, sometimes spreading over large parts of
her body. From the time she was six months old we had fought
this, trying every variation of diet and treatment we could
think of or that the doctors could suggest. There is no reason
to suppose that this trouble was caused by Lapland since the
same kind of allergies occur in many countries, particularly
the more developed countries.

During this time Lilian had slept very badly, at first not more
than half an hour at a time, and we had taken it in turns to
spend the night with her. At last she had begun to improve;
we thought that the worst days were over; then we found that
Henry had the same kind of skin and was suffering even more
than Lilian.

Henry had to be taken to hospital in Ivalo. Outside the hospital looked faded and worn; it had been put up immediately
after the war from whatever materials were available; but
inside it was clean, efficient, and friendly. The sister-in-charge
had a room on the left of the entrance; a waiting room was on
the right and a corridor ran crosswise with bedrooms on each
side and an X-ray room near the middle. Henry shared a room
with two other children. He spent most of his time with
greases and creams all over him and at night his hands had to
be tied to prevent his scratching his skin to pieces.

Eventually Henry came out of hospital and we continued his
treatment at home. Our household had changed. Before we
went to Helsinki, Fetsi had got married to a young man in the
forestry service; he had built a small house for them in that
residential area where the river curved round. Their marriage
had taken place one dull Sunday in the small Orthodox
Church. It was, at that time, not a proper church building at
all, but simply some rooms in a house on the eastern side of
Ivalo. It had been crowded when we went, the low ceilings
accentuating the denseness of the tightly packed black-coated
throng; through the dark coats and suits gleamed Fetsi's white
wedding dress and the green and gold of the priest's vestments,
the vestments which carried with them a faint lingering
memory of the glory of Byzantium and a thousand-year quarrel
over a word.

"Thank you," said Fetsi to us after the ceremony was over;
even at that unique time she remembered her English lessons.

Alli Junttila had also left and gone to Sweden; and in the
place of Alli and Fetsi we had Suoma, a girl in her teens who
came from Savukoski, still in Lapland, though south and east
of Ivalo, and an older woman from Inari. We always called

her "Aino *täti*", or "Aunt Aino". Aino *täti*, who was a good cook, was in charge of the domestic side of our affairs. Henry's need for attention at this time was so considerable that Arja needed full-time help with him. Suoma provided this. His treatment was also supervised by Sirkka-Liisa Hietala.

Sirkka-Liisa Hietala was Suoma's half-sister; she was the Parish Sister, that is to say she was employed by the Church to carry out nursing and welfare work in the parish. She was also the one woman member of the council. For a time she came in daily to put on Henry's dressings; and it was with her help and some specialist advice that we finally evolved the system which eventually cured Henry, though not for several months. This consisted of a mild cream put on night and day and covered with an opaque dressing to prevent evaporation, linked with the psychological therapy of almost continuous attention.

Heikki came to see Ilona from time to time, sometimes dressed in Lappish clothing: but mostly he was ski-ing after his reindeer in distant places. Once Ilona, coming from the telephone, said with a touch of pride: "Heikki has ski-ed forty kilometres to speak to me." She left about a month after we came back.

The darkness quietly retreated as the spring sun rose in the sky; and this spring I could ski—not gracefully, not fast, not so as to impress anybody, but knowing that if a tree was in the way I could guide myself round it and that if I needed to stop I was not limited to my bottom as the only brake. I would set out over the granulated snow in the afternoon, across the river and past the school into the forest where the bare birches drooped mournfully down, and in the distance the sunlight fell gold on the treetops and white on the snow-covered hills and appeared near to me as a million bright flashing points of light in the snow.

Sometimes when I returned late in the afternoon I would have a strange sensation: I would think of tea on an English lawn late on a summer's afternoon, and almost hear the tinkle of the cups before I realized that I was in silent Lapland gliding along the ski trail whilst the trees, dressed up with heavy blobs of snow, watched me like ghosts. I think it was the long shadows that gave the sudden illusion: for a moment they seemed the long shadows of summer and the mind caught at an old memory.

Being now two and a half, Lilian was, in Finnish eyes, quite ready to start ski-ing: and that spring she received her first pair of skis. There was a ski-ing competition for children one afternoon, with two classes: over four and under four. We felt, however, that perhaps she was a little too young for competition work.

The most exciting expedition of all, however, came in the middle of March: a winter visit to Pandy's. A summer visit to Pandy involved a journey up the lake; in winter reindeer had to be used. We went to Nellim first, there to meet a Lapp who was to provide reindeer and clothing and take us up to Pandy's house. The Lapp turned up, on time, with four reindeer and three sledges. These were not the light type of *pulkka* in which I had had my first ride, but the more substantial, flat-bottomed *kelkka*, which did not upset so easily and on which there was plenty of room to sit. Apart from one or two screws they were entirely wooden, including the runners. The shafts were tied on with leather.

The temperature was between minus ten and minus twenty Centigrade. I had not known how cold it would be and had put on the usual two pullovers and three pairs of socks in addition to *anorak*, ski trousers and long underwear. The Lapp had, however, brought us a *peski* each to wear. A *peski* looks more like a tent in reindeer hide than anything else. I put mine on over my head, then struggled towards a small patch of light I could see at the top, eventually emerging to find myself completely surrounded by reindeer hide and fur.

The *peski* is very warm; and to go with it were leggings. On my feet I had ski boots; and these were cold. The rest of me, however, was quite warm all day even though we were sitting on the sledge for several hours without much movement.

We started off, each in our own sledge and with our own reindeer. Arja, being a frail woman, had her reindeer tied to the leading sledge. Since I was a man the Lapp paid me the compliment of supposing that I knew how to drive a reindeer, and simply handed me the rein. This in itself was puzzling, since instead of having two reins, one to pull for left and one for right, there was only one rein on the left-hand side. I was left wondering how one could possibly turn to the right.

The reindeer showed no hesitation in starting off; we shot away, one after the other, down the slope which led out of the school, through the village and into the forest. The reindeer could corner fast, since they could put one foot down to stop themselves, and they went round as fast as they could with entire lack of concern to the sledge behind. This skidded round after the reindeer in a dizzy S.

I found myself surprised but still upright after the first corner; then we came to a sharp turn right with an alternative way straight ahead into a farm. The leading reindeer with

Arja's reindeer and sledge captive behind turned sharp right and raced merrily away. Mine walked calmly into the farmyard, stopped, and turned round and looked at me as though to say: "This is as far as we're going today, isn't it?"

I got off and pulled on its rein; nothing I could do would make it budge. Eventually two men from the farm turned it round; then the Lapp came back with a stick six to eight feet long. He said I was to hit the reindeer with this if it didn't go fast enough or in any other way misbehaved itself. He pointed the reindeer in the right direction; I gave it a sharp tap and we moved off again. In addition to standing obstinately still, the reindeer has an even more disturbing trick: that of starting off before you are really ready, so that you are either left behind completely or go sliding over the snow with the sledge beside instead of underneath you.

We went on peacefully for some time; I watched the white rear quarters and stumpy tail of the reindeer, black splotches of toes moving rhythmically to and fro, the diagonally opposite legs moving together and little ripples running first along one of its sides and then along the other. The road was very twisty and up and down at first, as it ran through the forest, and also very hard; and with nothing but one's clothing and solid wood between one and the ground, this hardness could be felt very clearly.

Then the track ran across lakes and islands, and became more smooth. Going across a lake once the road for no apparent reason swerved off its direct course and made an S-bend in the middle of the lake. I could think of no innocent explanation for this S-bend. My reindeer seemed to think the leader was going too fast; I hit it occasionally but had not the heart to do this very hard and we dropped steadily behind the others. However, we arrived at Pandy's still in sight of each other. It was strange to approach the house over what—the last time—had been liquid blue, and was now solid level white.

The reindeer rested whilst we went into Pandy's house and had coffee: behind them the trail stretched out, the one mark on the untouched snow, till it disappeared behind the trees on the horizon.

Pandy said that reindeer lived about fourteen years if female, twenty years if male, and thirty-five years if castrated. They shed their horns once a year, but each year the horns grew one more branch. Castrated reindeer shed their horns each year the same week as that in which they were castrated. The Lapps therefore castrated some reindeer in spring, some in summer, and so on. I asked Pandy if he thought that Lap-

Ivalo School from our house, with the Ivalo River in front

(*Above*) Repairs to the Menesjärvi road; our car waits for two planks to be put across the gap

(*Left*) Frying fish in the midnight sun

pish methods of killing reindeer were cruel. He said that a usual way to kill reindeer was to stick a knife in the vertebrae at the back of the neck as the reindeer raced round the enclosure. This stunned the reindeer, and it could then be killed. Done in this way the killing was not cruel; sometimes, however, a man would get drunk and then not be able to put in the knife quickly and accurately.

Pandy grumbled about the modern Ivalo. "It's not like it was before the war. In winter then there was a reindeer at each tree along the road in Ivalo, and most of the people in Lappish clothing."

Before the war, he said, the whole of northern Lapland was a Customs-free area. That explained the "Laanila Customs station" marked on the map, which had often puzzled me. It was south of Kaunispää, and quite a distance south from Ivalo: but in those pre-war days it was the first Customs barrier one met coming down from the Arctic. Tea and coffee brought by sea then cost much less than they did in southern Finland; now they are more expensive. Sugar also came that way; it was still possible, said Pandy, to see Tate and Lyle boxes dating from that time.

Pandy also showed me some greenish-coloured hay. This was used by the Lapps in their boots, he said; they did not wear socks.

When we set off back, my reindeer at once took the wrong direction and the rest of the party got ahead. I had now got some control over my beast, giving it a sharp flick against its side when I wanted to turn right, but we were still not entirely in harmony. For a time the others were out of sight; I was following the trail, but apart from that the world might have been totally uninhabited. The reindeer and I were a small dark spot in the middle of a lake, with nothing but blank snow till the eye reached a gap in the tree-lined horizon and saw through that a yet more distant line of trees. The horns of the reindeer move rhythmically up and down against a pearly-grey sky with a concealed sun lighting up long broad patches a faint gold.

There were strange noises in the sledge; swish, swish and rumble from the runners as they went over the hard snow, and queerer, less explicable phenomena—bursts of sound strangely reminiscent of a muffled jet plane or sports car horn.

The journey home took two or three hours, with my reindeer always very much in the rear. I hit it occasionally, and it speeded up for a time, then relapsed again into a comfortable amble. I did not like to be really firm with it; maybe I was a heavy load for it and why should it feel like pulling me fast

anyway? Not very far from Nellim, however, two female reindeer, loose, suddenly ran out of the forest and joined the party
immediately behind Arja's sledge. My reindeer was a male;
and as soon as it saw the two girls its attitude to life changed
completely. It raced after the others enthusiastically, we
hurtled down the hill past the farm, round the corner hell-for-
leather and came to a stop outside the school with two reindeer
more than we had started out with. It is, surely, untrue to say
that animals never have the same thoughts and feelings as
human beings.

16 : Roads and Cars

WE FELL, that spring, for the temptation. I had stood against it up to that time both because I thought the more primitive methods were better for us, and also because, having had experience, I knew how much it would cost. But that April we fell. We bought a car.

Tane, the Utsjoki Police representative, was the instrument of our fall. He arrived from Utsjoki one day and began talking about cars. He owned a Morris Minor which he kept in impeccable condition; he said it was still worth 500,000 marks (about £550) although it was five years old. Since Tane had to travel over some of the roughest roads of the commune, this was a considerable recommendation. He also said that he had heard that two new Morris Minor 1000 cars had just arrived in Rovaniemi. They were for sale, but were not likely to remain so for long.

We had, to be honest, already opened the road to temptation ourselves. We had considered the possibility of getting a car and even started to make inquiries. That, in Finland, was a complicated business, since there were all the cars of the world to choose from—though not all on the same terms. American Chevrolets, Russian Pobedas and the West German Mercedes Benz stood side by side on the taxi rank in Ivalo; our landlord's son ran a Czechoslovakian Skoda; and the Ivalo health sister owned an East German Wartburg. We had already been offered a second-hand French Peugeot and a Ford.

Petrol, too, came from various sources: we had the choice of Shell, Esso, Gulf, and TB. The two last letters stood for the "Benzine Free Trust Company". This imported petrol from Russia. The second-hand value of the cars, however, varied considerably. The British cars kept their value very well, but the eastern cars dropped off enormously after a year or two. In buying a British car, also, it was necessary to pay cash down, or someone else would take it. The eastern cars could, however, usually be obtained on credit terms extending over a year or two. Those who owned a Moskvitch were usually rather apologetic.

Arja was on her way to Rovaniemi for a couple of days. She looked at me.

"I'll come too," I said. "We'll have a look at this car. We don't need to buy it even then."

That evening, however, in our bedroom in Hotel Pohjanhovi, we were calculating how to raise the necessary money and
ringing up the bank manager in Ivalo. A day or two later we
were in the centre of Rovaniemi with our own car and nothing
between us and home except 180 miles of snow-covered
road.

Rovaniemi was almost completely destroyed during the war,
and has been entirely rebuilt. The hotel where we stayed,
Pohjanhovi, "The Court of the North", had sixty modern
rooms, about half with their own bathroom. In the restaurant
one had the choice of dancing; eating the Lapland delicacies
such as reindeer tongue and, in season, elk; or staring out at
the waters rushing past below, where the Ounasjoki and
Kemijoki joined and went rolling down to the Gulf of Bothnia.

To the west of the river the houses stretched out, neat and
white, though with an isolated look as though the streets were
not yet complete; and on the other bank of the river, past the
hospital, rose the heights of Ounasvaara. On top of Ounasvaara
was a ski-ers' hostel and a tall radio mast, with a little building
by the side of the mast. This was the northern limit, at that
time, of Finland's very-high-frequency radio system; this has
since been extended to cover the whole of the country.

The map of Rovaniemi was not entirely accurate; it showed
streets which had been planned but abandoned. It is true in
Finland generally and in Lapland in particular that it is difficult to find a map showing all the existing roads accurately. It
indicates the rate at which roads are being built—they have
got ahead of the maps.

This was Rovaniemi, the administrative centre of Lapland.
"The Gateway to Lapland" it called itself on the posters; but
we always thought of it as the gateway to the south. For many
Rovaniemi was the gateway also to alcohol. For most people
north of it Rovaniemi was the nearest place at which alcohol
could be bought for home consumption. To find the alcohol
stores it was only necessary to look for the queue, which usually
stretched out of the door and down the street.

We drove across the long new bridge which spanned the
river where it ran through the town and a few minutes later
across the other bridge which spanned the Kemijoki. This
second bridge was not so commodious at the first one. Road
and rail both shared the same few feet of width, so that the car
had to go along the railway line. There are many unguarded
level crossings in Finland, none of which I like, but these crossings where one has to travel over a river along a railway line I
like least of all, guarded or unguarded. We reached the other

side and made sure a few kilometres further on that we took
the left turn, to the north, and not the right one towards Russia.
After that it was difficult to make a mistake; there was no other
major road before Sodankylä.

We journeyed slowly and carefully on along the white
traffic-less road, through Sodankylä, through Vuotso, over
Kaunispää, gleaming white in the moonlight, until finally,
long after dark had fallen we reached Ivalo safely—and got
stuck on our own front drive. Snow had been falling on the
drive all through the winter; it had been cleared away, more
or less, but there was a lot of soft stuff piled on each side of a
narrow track and when the car went into this it could not get
out. It remained ignominiously there until put back on the
track by two strong frontier guard patients the following
morning.

Driving is possible on the main roads of Lapland throughout
the year. The worst time is in the spring and autumn when
the temperature is around zero and the snow is melting or not
thoroughly frozen. In spring there are frequent patches of mud
through which the car swerves unsteadily; and the most skiddy
surface is that produced by frozen ice with rain on top. When
the temperature falls to minus ten Centigrade or below the
road grips much better, and below minus twenty it is—as
they say—"as good as a summer surface". There was no day
whilst we were there when the road to Rovaniemi was not
passable, but once or twice it needed an expert driver to get
through.

Most cars fit either two or four winter tyres at the beginning
of winter; chains are only used by the heavy vehicles under the
worst conditions.

A somewhat disturbing discovery was now made on the
administrative side. I had for many years held an English
driving licence and I had hoped that this—perhaps combined
with an International Driving Permit or some other document
which could be obtained merely on paying a fee—would be
sufficient. It now appeared that, since I was a more or less permanent resident of Finland, I ought to hold a Finnish licence
and for this purpose pass a Finnish test. No one was very hurried about it; it was just suggested that if I wanted to drive
outside Inari commune I ought, some time, to put this matter
in order.

I waited till the snow had vanished; then we went to
Rovaniemi again. This time we lived more economically: we
stayed in a *matkustajakoti* and ate in various kinds of *baari*. A
matkustajakoti—"traveller's home"—generally provides good

clean single or double rooms with running water but not much beyond tea or coffee by way of food. A *baari*—"bar"—usually cannot sell alcohol but provides tea, coffee, soft drinks and also quite good food. This is a much cheaper existence than sleeping and eating solely in hotels; one must, however, recognize that whilst English is spoken in most of the hotels, it is much more rarely spoken in the *baari* and the *matkustajakoti*.

Rovaniemi had for a long time been able to provide the first-class standard, with its accompanying expense, but had only recently developed places which provided a simpler but still satisfactory service. It was well for us that it had done; since getting the car we had had no spare money and had taken our credit as far as we felt it ought to go.

We were in one especial difficulty with the test: it was necessary to take it in a car bigger than the one we owned. There was, however, a very friendly atmosphere about the Vanhanen motor business, from which we had bought the Morris. Vanhanen treated his customers and their cars as though they were a real personal concern of his. There was always some coffee ready when we called in; and as soon as he knew of our trouble over the test he offered to lend us a bigger car free of charge.

It would have been extremely embarrassing to have failed the test—being theoretically an experienced driver—and a Finnish test is a thoroughgoing experience. The driver must first pass a medical examination, then in addition to the practical test on the road he may be asked questions both on the technical functioning of the car and on Finnish road signs and motoring law. Road signs are fortunately fairly international, the most individual exception being the frequent Finnish sign in spring and autumn:

KELIRIKKO—"road broken".

We set off in the car with the examiner and my wife; I drove some way and turned a corner, wondering what he was thinking. Then I heard him say to my wife in Finnish:

"This man drives well."

What an examiner! What an examiner!

The car, however, even though I now possessed double authority to drive it, did not confine me entirely to the life of the road. There were still discoveries to be made away from it. An event that led to one of them arrived quite unexpectedly. I was working at my desk in the surgery one morning when a patient came in. I gave him a casual glance and put my head down when suddenly my ear caught a name.

Crottet? Had he said Crottet?

He had, so it appeared; he was Robert Crottet—the writer who lived in Switzerland and who at the end of the war had done so much to rouse interest in the Kolta Lapps.

Crottet was an elusive figure; he would come unexpectedly to Lapland, appearing occasionally in Ivalo but spending most of the time in out-of-the-way spots with his friends, the Kolta Lapps. He would disappear as suddenly as he had come. He was interested, not so much in the way the Kolta Lapps kept reindeer, as in their dreams. He was staying with one of the very oldest of the Kolta Lapps, Kaisa, and he invited me to go one day to meet her.

It was a June day; the roads were clear but the snow was reluctant to leave and a little was still falling. I drove out half-way to Nellim, then stopped by the side of a lake. Crottet was waiting with a boat, and we set out rowing across it. There was still ice on the lake. It was not as warm as I had expected; the temperature was down to minus two Centigrade, and my hands froze as the boat moved through the water and the day shone with a clear, cold beauty. A black cat watched us elegantly as we landed and walked up to the little house which Kaisa's sons had built.

The rooms inside were small, but very warm and homely. Kaisa was a small, exquisite grey-haired figure. She was eighty; she had been born in the days when Finland was part of Russia, and she herself spoke Russian as well as Finnish. She had the dignity of an aristocrat.

Crottet believed that Kaisa might have some foreknowledge of the future: he told me that she had known when the last war would begin. "She says that there will be no war until the year 2000, and that then China will attack the whole of Europe, and Russia." He smiled. "And she's never wrong."

Crottet also had another guest: a young man who came from a well-known Lappish family—not Kolta Lappish—and whose home was between Inari and Utsjoki. He was at the University in Helsinki; Crottet thought he might one day become a writer.

There were, at that time, two Finnish Lapps who were receiving University education. The number is partly a matter of chance; it might have been none or it might have been more. At first sight it looks very small; but two out of 2,500—the approximate number of Finnish Lapps—is equivalent to 40,000 out of a population of 50,000,000, which is approximately the number of University students in Britain before the war.

It would, therefore, be wrong to regard the Lapps as a people incapable of attaining a high educational standard. In Inari commune a child could take his education as far as the end of middle school, corresponding to an age of about sixteen. To go up to the standard needed for University entrance he would have to leave Inari commune and go to Rovaniemi. A bright Lapp child might be intellectually suitable for a University education but unable to stand the expense.

Not all, however, wanted such an education even amongst those who were suitable. One Lapp boy came to the Head of the Middle School for advice: what was it like being in her position, he asked? What had one to do to get there? She told him, and he thought it over.

"Being a reindeer man is the best work, of course," he said. "But if one couldn't be a reindeer man then your work might be quite good."

The boy belonged to a very able family of considerable standing; it is quite possible that he could have become qualified in an academic profession if he had been determined to do this. But it is also possible that he would be happier and have more time for thinking, and more freedom to think independently, as a reindeer man.

Lapp families were by no means all of one standard. Some were poor; one or two were comparatively rich. The average reindeer owner had less than a hundred reindeer; perhaps ten or twenty men in the commune owned several hundred, and one or two over a thousand. At the bottom end of the scale those who only had a few dozen reindeer would have to supplement their income by other work; and at the top end, if the average value of a reindeer were between five and ten thousand marks (five to ten pounds), at least one or two men possessed an appreciable capital—even though most of it was wandering on the hills. Some Lapps complained that the banks were not ready enough to recognize this as a security, despite its considerable value.

According to Finnish law, any Finnish national living in Lapland may own reindeer. This differs from Norway and Sweden, in which reindeer herding is a Lapp monopoly. In Finland less than a quarter of the total number of reindeer were in Lapp hands. The average number owned per Finn, however, was very much smaller than the average number per Lapp; for the Finns, reindeer keeping was essentially only a part-time occupation.

I asked the young man in Kaisa's house what he thought about the relations between the Lapps and the Finns. He shrugged his shoulders.

"This contact has gone on so long," he said, "I suppose it must continue now."

It was plain that he regarded the Lapps as a separate group of which he was a member and not as a group which ought to be absorbed by the Finns. The educated Lapp, however, must face many problems. He may feel a sense of insecurity, of not belonging anywhere. If he or she returns to Lapland, the Lapps themselves may be reluctant to accept one of their own race as belonging to an apparently superior educated class. When one professional appointment was being made some Lapps said that they would prefer a Finn in it. The problem, therefore, of preserving a Lapp culture led by Lapps is not a straightforward one.

I drove back from the visit to Kaisa's in daylight; though the weather was cold the days were long. It was a brilliant summer; but how short the Lapland summer could be! There had been ice on the lake when I visited Kaisa; the summer had scarcely begun; and yet by the ninth of August there was a touch of autumn in the air and the temperature fell to only one degree above freezing point. It was not like that every day; a week later the summer returned and the temperature rose to over twenty Centigrade; but one could not forget the winter for long.

During this second burst of summer we went to Utsjoki again, with Eeva Ruuskanen, a friend from Helsinki. This time we went by the new road. It was still a very rough road; the sharp stones flew from under the wheels of the car and one could rarely travel comfortably at more than twenty-five miles an hour; but it had altered that whole character of the district. The path seemed to have shrunk back into the forest, and that inaccessible, lonely beauty could now be reached by bus which ran several times a week from Inari to Utsjoki.

It was still a very beautiful way, even though the wounds which the road had made in the forest had not healed and the stones lay scattered along its edges, not yet covered by grass or moss. It was a road of different moods: first the sombreness of the marshes; then the rise over the hills and the first sight of the Norwegian mountains in the distance; and finally the narrow ridges, falling sharply down to water on either side, and the sharp turn along a cliff edge just before Utsjoki with the sign in four languages:

DANGER: FALLING STONES
DRIVERS USE THIS ROAD AT THEIR OWN RISK

There was a division of opinion in the Utsjoki commune

as to whether this road ought to be built or not. Utsjoki is the most Lappish commune, and some of the Lapps thought this interfered with the Lappish way of life, which is essentially lived away from the road. They also said, with reason, that the road would bring too many tourists who would take fish for pleasure which they needed for their livelihood; and the tourists frequently had more expensive and better fishing equipment.

We drove on through Utsjoki, warm and still in the afternoon sun, to the road leading to the river. There was now a full-blooded Customs station in Utsjoki, with a bar across the road; we stopped and were examined, then drove to the river's edge. There was no bridge, but a ferry; once on the Norwegian side there was no Customs and no further formalities, nothing but some miles of rough going and then an adequate road right to the coast.

Just past Utsjoki the road climbed high above the river. We stopped the car and lay on the grass, gazing at the river and at Finland. Below was a *köngäs*—rapids where the water rolled incessantly over the rocks with a distant powerful roaring. Long thin lines of foam struck across the blue, and on the opposite side the hills stood transfixed in the sunlight.

It was a rare, sharply happy moment; the kind of moment that came to me sometimes in Lapland, though even there, not very often; a moment when perception suddenly heightened, when one was conscious of the inexpressible.

The mountains stood out against the evening sky as we neared the northern edge of Norway. The country was filled with farm animals; indeed, they seemed to own it. There were fences all along the road, but the animals were invariably on the road side of the fence. Cows, horses, and sheep watched us go past or reluctantly got up off the road and made way. We had booked rooms, blindly, at Hotel Brakka; we had failed to realize that *brakka* meant "barracks". The hotel, when we reached it, was not what we had expected; it was so little like what we had expected that we immediately fled, seeking out rooms wherever they could be found.

The mountain roads of Norway, though twisty, were not as difficult as expected. Traffic was light, and no awkward situations arose in passing other vehicles. We drove along a high upland road, above the tree line, with low green vegetation rolling away on either side. We stopped, in the evening, near the sea. The sun had almost set; on the water one small boat sailed towards the purple and gold reflections of the sky. But it was the mountains behind us that were most remarkable: they were washed in a pink, not a dead colour but a living one, as though they were translucent and revealing a fire within. In a few moments, as we watched, the pink deepened to red, then the red to purple, purple to violet, and the violet slowly sank into the dark blue of night.

We stayed that night in Lakselv, and continued the next day to Karasjok, still in Norway, with the road running through glorious mountain scenery—and a military area slap across the road in the best part. It extended on either side, with notices forbidding camping and a truck which ran up to watch anyone who stopped to look at the mountains. It ended, neatly, as soon as the scenery became flatter and less interesting. Notices warned the visitor that this superb spot was not for him; they were in several languages including Lappish, though not, as far as I could see, Russian.

Eeva had left us in Lakselv, and gone off to North Cape— a few hours away and the extreme northern point of Europe.

We halted in Karasjok, just on the Norwegian side of the border with Finland. Many people came here from Ivalo to buy margarine; it was only two or three hours in a car and the Norwegian margarine was very good and cheap. The road dropped down from the sparse vegetation of the moors to the village, standing like an oasis in the river valley below. With its Lapp schools, museum, old church and tradition as a meeting-place for the mountain Lapps, Karasjok would have been a good starting point for a study of Lapp life in Norway. It was, however, actually nearer to the capital of Finland than of its own country: 1,340 miles to Oslo, but only 890 to Helsinki.

Lilian ran to meet us as the car pulled up outside our home. She loved to travel, and on shorter trips she was usually taken along. She often went to our *kämppä* and also once or twice to one which Eetu and Maija Saarelainen had recently acquired.

This had the added romance of being on an island. It had originally been a disused hut belonging to the Forest Administration, in quite a different place. Eetu had bought it and had it taken to the island over the ice during the winter.

One Saturday we drove along the Inari road for about ten kilometres, then pulled up by the water's edge. Eetu kept his boat in the grasses near the water; we got in and rowed across to the island. It was one island out of very many, yet each had its own character. It was not a very big island, just a nice cosy size which took a few minutes to walk round. It was covered with trees, and between the trees at this time of the year berries in abundance were to be had for the picking. On the edge remote from the road was the hut; this was divided into two parts. In one was just room to live and sleep; in the other was the *sauna*.

We spent the day there, picking berries, cleaning the fish which Eetu had caught, having *sauna*, watching the reflection of the forest in the lake, and having coffee: freedom and peace. Without understanding this kind of holiday it is impossible to understand the Finns. One can spend the same sort of hours and days and weeks on an island in southern Finland—but in Lapland the experience is most complete.

When we rowed back it was already dark: we were returning home but Eetu and Maija were going to stay overnight on the island.

"Daddy," said Lilian when we reached home, "shall we go to the island tomorrow?" All day she had been completely happy carrying water up and down and pouring it from bucket to bucket on the beach outside the hut.

"Not tomorrow, I'm afraid."

"But *some time*?" There was such a wealth of wistful longing in her voice.

"Oh yes. We'll go there again some time. Was it nice?"

"*It was.*"

She went to bed then, contented, and I was left thinking of the moment when we had parted from Eetu and Maija, we going to our car and they rowing back whilst the moon drew a long silvery path on the water, the dark shape of the boat becoming smaller and smaller and the sound of the oars more and more faint as they went towards the island.

17 : The Flames of Autumn

THAT was a hellish summer for mosquitoes. Mosquitoes are prolific in Lapland; they are worst at the end of June and in July, then in August the numbers fall off. They do not carry disease, but they are a terrible nuisance. The weather can be very warm in the middle of summer, but because of these tiny devils it is still necessary to wear thick clothing. Mosquito oil protects, but not always completely. At the end of June and in July Lapland is at its lightest and warmest; the earth is flourishing; but so also are the mosquitoes. At the end of August the evenings are colder and the days are shorter; but the mosquitoes have lost their grip, and this is a good time for walking.

Kalle said the mosquitoes never bit a heavy drinker; they couldn't stand the alcohol in the bloodstream.

They reached a peak of intensity during one week in which we had to put nets over the children's beds. The mosquitoes settled down for a little while in the early hours of the morning; but they were waiting, lined up on the wall, and as soon as we woke they took off like a dawn patrol.

The children's Lapland days, however, were numbered; and so were ours. We had decided to leave in the autumn of that year. Why did that time seem the right one to leave? We had stayed far longer than we originally intended; it was not possible for me to support the family adequately in Lapland and from that point of view it was necessary to leave as soon as possible. Before that time, however, there would have been something lacking. It was only that autumn that I came to the end of the final version of the book, and only during that last summer did we get a complete impression of Lapland. Even this impression only made us realize how much more there was still to explore; what wonderful, peaceful holidays might be spent if we should return.

I wanted, if possible, to have my cake and eat it, to keep one foot in electronics and yet to develop the life of the imagination, of feeling and expression, of those non-material things which flutter round us and at which we catch in the darkness. If, however, an ultimate choice had to be made, it was clear which way it had to be made. I had learned to distrust an action, however expedient it appeared, if it disagreed with my own inner perception.

157

When the inner struggles are resolved, practical means often open up. I had been offered a temporary appointment at Viittakivi, at which I had taught English the same summer that we were married. This was a foothold in the world of the south; it gave me considerable freedom in lecturing and a number of hours teaching English. The teaching of English to Finns I had now come to regard as both important and satisfying.

With me I was going to take something else: the knowledge that a primitive culture could be peaceful, could be happy, and might offer to man's spirit a greater satisfaction than our own. The strains and dissatisfactions in our own culture were not inherent in life; there were answers to them, but to find those answers we should have to look outside our own culture.

Our next home was to be seven hundred miles further south, near the village of Hauho. When we went to Lapland we thought that we should need only a few little bits of furniture, the minimum necessary for a few months; we seemed in fact to have acquired a cumbrous collection of property, not all of it very portable. We decided to send the children first, with Suoma, to their grandmother in Helsinki for a few weeks whilst we finished off what had to be done in Ivalo.

We set out with the children for Rovaniemi one September morning. At that time of the year the road, though unsurfaced, was in good condition; we drove at a steady forty or fifty miles an hour whilst the children, sitting in the back with Suoma, dropped off to sleep, one little head nodding one way and one the other. We stopped to see Heikki and Ilona, now both in Sodankylä. It was a very worthwhile stop, for—apart from the pleasure of seeing friends—Heikki gave us some reindeer meat. Being a reindeer man he had selected the very best parts, which were delicious. We reached the airport at Rovaniemi, wondering how Henry, still only nine months old, would bear this long journey of five and a half hours by road and four hours by plane. But suddenly Henry, propped up on a bench against the wall, lifted up his head and laughed as though the whole world were a wonderful joke. It seemed a good omen.

After the others had gone I went in the car to Kemi. Arja took the children to Helsinki and saw them safely settled before returning to the north. We now had only a few weeks to see all we wanted to see in Lapland. We intended to return to Ivalo by a long route, going into Sweden and making a sweep round through north Norway. We expected the trip to be interesting, but we could not guess, then, just how fortunate we were going to be.

Kemi, which had a population of over 20,000—more than Rovaniemi—was supposed to be one of the strongholds of Communism in Lapland. This was a different world, a world of saw mills, sulphate and cellulose factories, and the powerful Kemijoki River, the whole area through which the road ran looking—compared with northern Lapland—settled and tamed and owned. Kemi was a mixed town; some of the side streets were lined with pleasantly old-fashioned wooden houses; but straight through the centre ran a broad highway with sleek efficient modern buildings on each side, dominated by a ten-storey block with a clock on top. The road with its width and its careful grouping signs was so impressive that I flinched as I drove into the centre of the town, expecting a flood of traffic to come roaring at me. Either it was a quiet time, or the road was built for the future; there were only one or two cars and a bus to be seen.

I stayed overnight in a *matkustajakoti*; it had a heavy Victorian air, but was quite comfortable. The next day Arja joined me, and we set out for the border towns of Tornio and Haparanda. The western border of Finland is a long river valley, the river being the Muoniojoki in the north and the Torniojoki in the south. It includes beautiful hill, water, and forest scenery. Its character is, however, different from the east. The border river may be crossed easily at several places, so the whole region is closely in contact with Sweden—not surrounded by Finnish territory like Ivalo. It has several tourist centres which are usually heavily booked during the peak holiday season.

Tornio is an ancient township, connected by rail with both Sweden and Finland. Most of it is on an island, joined by a bridge to the mainland. Alatornio—*ala* means "lower"—was the place which in earlier times was the base of the *pirkkalaiset*—the first Finnish settlers in Lapland. From here they made their expeditions into the interior. They had the right of trading with the Lapps and also of collecting taxes from them. Whilst the Lapps may have been to some extent oppressed, they always had the defence of simply not turning up to meet the tax collector: a defence not so easy to use in modern civilization.

There is a road up the valley on either side of the river, one in Finland and one in Sweden. We decided that for the first part of the journey we would travel on the Swedish side, crossing back again farther north. We left Tornio, passed the Customs, and swerved to the left on the bridge to the west: then we were in Sweden, fabulous Sweden, with superb coffee, excellent roads, and smart clothing. Looked at from Finland, we felt that Sweden was a land of luxuries; we looked at the luxuries with a slight touch of envy, but also with a feeling of pride that we could do without them, or at least paid more for them.

The Swedish road was undoubtedly good, by northern standards; it was very thoroughly and carefully marked, especially with passing places. We wanted to go as far as we could that day, so kept on driving until nightfall. We stopped in a village we didn't know at all and looked round for somewhere to stay. A strange village in a strange country after dark is a mysterious place; it feels at one and the same time dead and shut up, and throbbing with secret life. We saw a hotel; it seemed to have no door but a back door, and a very dingy outside appearance. With memories of Hotel Brakka, we rejected it. This was a mistake; when, after having obtained some simple accommodation in a house, we returned to the hotel and boldly walked in, we found a very pleasant, cosy dining-room.

We set off again in the morning, after an early breakfast of coffee and freshly baked rolls in a Konditori in the village, which now seemed friendly and open and kind-hearted as it woke up in the morning sun. We planned to cross the river at Muonio. Muonio is a road junction; the road up the valley from Tornio here meets the road coming across from Rovaniemi. It is near to the Pallastunturi hills; the attractive "tourist inn" on Pallastunturi is very popular both during the ski-ing season and in the summer. Muonio is on the Finnish side; and we had been told that there was a new bridge across the river to it. When we came to the river, however, the road simply ran down into the water, with no sign of any bridge and only a boat far too small to take a car. Arja inquired in a shop at the end of the road; there had apparently been some misunderstanding and the new bridge was only going to be built in two years. It was too long to wait, so we turned back and headed northwards for Karesuando where we knew for certain there was a way across.

At this point I nearly wiped us out.

As we returned along the road we met a small van. I moved over to let him pass, and he moved over too, but in the same direction. I moved to one side as far as I could, and he did the same so that we still faced each other.

"The man's mad!" I thought, and then suddenly realized —we were still in Sweden, not in Finland.

Swedish traffic is on the left, Finnish and Norwegian on the right. Going into Sweden I had at first driven rather carefully, then I realized that given the appropriate warning my inner control mechanism simply switched over. But at Muonio I had unconsciously set myself for Finland and right-hand traffic— and forgotten to make the necessary change when we turned back into Sweden.

We crossed into Finland at Karesuando (or Kaaresuvanto). Along this border between Finland and Sweden there are a succession of villages, or small towns, which have a counter-part immediately opposite them in the other country. At Muonio the Finnish village was by far the bigger; at Kare-suando there was more on the Swedish side. We were now in Enontekio, Finland's most north-westerly commune, in which the country rose in the north to heights of 4,000 feet or so, higher than elsewhere in Lapland. The Lapps here were the *tunturi* or "mountain" Lapps; of the Lapps they were the most nearly nomadic.

Darkness fell as we headed north towards Kilpisjärvi; I had just time to notice a sign at the edge of the road as it shone in the glare of the headlights and then disappeared behind. There was silence for a moment in the car, then:

"What do you think that sign was?" asked Arja.

"I thought it said: ROAD WORK FOR 25 KILOMETRES."

"So did I. It must have said two-point-five kilometres. We must be wrong."

"We must be wrong."

But we were not wrong, and for fifteen miles we ploughed slowly along over the stones and irregularities. Round us Lapland seemed very big and very dark. In the end, however, there was the gleam of light on a lake, a road sign pointing to the left, and we were at Kilpisjärvi.

Kilpisjärvi consists of one or two houses and a shop, and the Kilpisjärvi hotel with its associated buildings. The hotel is a first-class modern hotel with comfortable bedrooms and a big restaurant, serving good food throughout the day and even prepared to lash something together at unheard-of hours like five o'clock in the morning when an early bus leaves. One can drive up this road, stay at Kilpisjärvi, and see Lapland in luxury. Part of Lapland, that is; to see something of the Lapland of the wilderness one must leave the road behind.

One could reach either Kilpisjärvi or Ivalo without abandoning much of one's civilized ways; if one walked across from Kilpisjärvi to Ivalo, where there is no road but only paths over the mountains and through the forest, that would be quite a different experience. It would not, however, be good to try this without knowing exactly where one was going and without proper preparation and equipment. Apart from this, however, there are a number of marked trails with overnight huts, and accommodation is not restricted to hotels. At Kilpisjärvi there were also much cheaper hostel and camping facilities. Once having reached Lapland, a holiday for the out-of-door type can be quite cheap.

At this time we began to realize how lucky we had been. It was the *ruska* time, the season when the brilliant autumn colours suddenly flared across the landscape. But *ruska* is short lived, only at its best for two or three weeks, and these best weeks are not the same each year. Every year, too, *ruska* is not the same: the cold must come before the wet, so that the dead leaves are sharp and brilliant, not damp and dull. *Ruska*, at its height, is a difficult thing to see if one lives outside Lapland; one may be a week too early or too late; or that year the *ruska* may be only indifferent.

But we were lucky—it was a good year for *ruska* and we had come at the right time. I realized this when I woke in the morning and walked on to the balcony outside the bedroom. A tide of clear yellow rolled over the land, with the lake a long splash in the middle; in the distance, over the water, the snow glistened on the peaks of Sweden; and behind was Saana, one of Finland's highest mountains, rising in a smooth flattened purple curve against the sky.

We climbed Saana that day. As we stood on top, looking across to Saana's eternal companion, Malla, on the other side of the road, we seemed to stand at a peak in time, in the year— in the distance was the white of winter, coming over the mountain tops; yet down below the summer was still there, flaring up in a final hectic brilliance. It was lonely country, rolling away into the distance with only the great shining pools breaking it up; but now the unending, intimidating green of spring and summer and the all-conquering white of winter were neither present. Instead, a warmth crept out from the earth and diffused itself over the whole landscape.

We drove on into Norway the next day; it was like the morning of the world, clear, sharp, full of promise. One of the beauties of *ruska* is the contrast of colour—the uncompromisingly yellow birches standing beside the stark dark green of the pines, a branch of mountain ash the colour of blood against an azure sky.

Ahead were the mountains, promising new revelations of light and hue; and then we were amongst them—and not only the mountains but the water. The mountains were not one, but two—one going up to the sky, and the other a liquid mountain dropping into the depths of the water.

We travelled along the coast of north Norway, a coast not for the impatient, with its irregularities and sudden inlets round which one had to travel—but how foolish to be impatient in such golden days. This north Norway appealed to me immensely, with its combination of mountain and sea and clear air; and Norwegian has a very friendly sound to anyone who has lived in the north of England.

It was a little ironical that at that time of the year, one of the best times of all, accommodation was very easy to find. We stopped where it was convenient. We did, however, like to be in before nightfall. The roads were not difficult in daylight; but they were steep, and they were twisty, and there were some quite big drops. Norwegian roads were marked, but much less than the Swedish ones. They indicated the corners; after having travelled for miles along a road which was continuously curving from one side to the other, one would suddenly come across a notice saying: BEND. It was worth putting there; a bend marked as a bend in north Norway was curved enough to satisfy anybody. Between Arja and myself, the phrase "a Norwegian bend" came to mean a real bend, round which there was no doubt whatever one ought to slow down.

We crossed the ferry between Lyngen and Olderdalen in the late afternoon—a pleasant break from driving, a smooth trip of an hour or so across the head of a fjord watching the mountains on the opposite side steadily growing larger—drove on for an hour or two and finally pulled up in a waterside village where we stayed at an inn which had a very clubby British sort of atmosphere. (But apparently not double windows. The winter must have been warmer here—that would have been impossible in Inari.) The food, unfortunately, was not so good; *smörgasbord*, the miscellany of help-yourself dishes, for dinner, and *smörgasbord* again for breakfast. *Smörgasbord* can be a most wonderful meal; but it can also be nothing more than a few tins, and after the second of such meals I began to have inner doubts.

It is only fair to say that most of the food in Norway was very good. On the next day we had a really first-class mid-day meal at a *gestgiveri,* tender meat with three vegetables and an excellent fruit pie and custard to finish. The only cloud in the sky was that the day was Sunday, nowhere in which it was possible to change money was open, and we were anxiously watching our Norwegian money to see if it would last out.

Just before darkness came the colours changed, a deep

purple tinge overcoming them; and in the water were the reflections of the evening sky. Once in this evening light we passed a mountain down from which a stream was rushing; we could see each curve as it came, right from the top to the bottom.

We reached the boundary of Norway and Finland with a little in hand, and slowed down as we approached the Norwegian Customs post. The officer was outside; he saw us, smiled, and waved his hand towards Finland. The bar was up and we did not even need to stop. There was one change in our method of driving on the road home from the border to Ivalo: for most of the way Arja took the wheel. She was learning to drive. According to Finnish law this can only be done at a driving school or in the care of an authorized instructor; in the towns it is necessary to go to a driving school, but in remote country areas it is possible for a private individual to get permission to be the learner's official teacher. I had this permission, signed by Kalle, and as soon as we were in his administrative area, we used it.

We had seen the *ruska* of the mountains and the trees; perhaps it was only more slowly, as one studied it carefully, that one realized the other glory of *ruska* time: the ground. City-bred, the eyes instinctively kept away from the surface beneath them which had so often been dull or dirty. At last, when one looked, one saw that the earth was, if anything, more varied in colour than the rest, and as bright. There were the cool colours in it, light green and white; there were the dark colours of the rocks; but there were also the warm colours, browns and yellows and shades of red. They blended together into a pattern, a pattern lovely to look at; yet some of the details were even more striking—bright red moss against dark hard rock, looking as though it sprang from the rock itself. The ground kept its colours the longest; they stayed till the snow came and added a sprinkling of white to the red and the green.

The house seemed very quiet without the children, and sometimes I could almost see the phantasm of a little girl shrieking with laughter as she ran round and round between living room and kitchen. They were now in Helsinki; in a few weeks we should join them; and here in Ivalo the line between day and night was moving steadily across the evening.

Whilst there was still light for walking we made one more expedition into the forest. This was to Pielpajärvi Church. Pielpajärvi Church was the old church of Inari commune, built in 1760. It is now off the main routes, and surrounded by forest and lakes. It is disused, except for a service held once a year. On the map there is (apparently) a straightforward path from Inari to Pielpajärvi.

This was, to be honest, our second expedition to Pielpajärvi. Our first journey, or attempted journey, had been on midsummer day to attend the yearly service. Many people went to this from all parts of the district; one way to reach the church was to go by a special boat which sailed from Inari to a point about a mile from the church. Failing this, one could walk from Inari to Pielpajärvi, a distance of about seven kilometres or four miles.

We reached Inari a little late for the boat, which was sailing out as we reached the lake. So we drove the car to the Lappish Folk High School nearby, which was as far in that direction as the road went, and set out to walk. The way was so plainly marked on the map that we thought there would be little difficulty. We passed one or two houses, then after that there was nothing but forest.

It was pleasant walking through the forest. After some time we came to a point where the paths divided; we went alongside a lake, then across a narrow strip of land. We then found we could go no farther: we were on an island. We had quite clearly gone wrong.

We never found the church that day. We retraced our steps and tried a different path; we spent the morning and afternoon walking through the forest; once in the distance we heard voices, but we never saw a soul. That was all on a small corner of the map near Inari, which looked to have a clear path marked across it. This sort of experience makes one realize how empty Lapland is; and it gives one an increased respect for the Lapps who are never lost in it.

This second time, in the autumn, we went with two or three others and a guide who took us confidently straight to the church. It stood in a clearing not very far from a lake, a simple wooden building 200 years old.

"But why here?" I asked. "In the middle of the wilderness?"

"Because it was in the most central position. The routes have changed."

Round the church were the remains of storehouses and other provision for limited farming; the pastor in those days would have had to be to a large extent self-supporting, and also self-protecting, since bears and wolves were all around, then, and not merely in the remotest spots as now. We went inside. The fading daylight crept through the windows on to the plain wooden seats and pulpit; the church was filled at once with gloom, a gloom which had in it something of the forest and the fading autumn, and expectancy. One could imagine the congregation of an earlier day after their long hard journey, waiting for the flash of light in the darkness.

The old burial ground of the Lapps, once on land, had been moved out to an island—Ukonsaari. The reason for this was to protect the bodies from bears, which otherwise came and dug them up.

We hurried back in order to reach Inari before dark. It would not be long now before the winter.

18: Last Journeyings

BY FINNISH law all children living more than five kilometres from a school have to be provided with board and lodging at the school, or equivalent facilities. Since the homes of children in Lapland may be up to sixty kilometres from the school, a great many of them lived during term time in the *asuntola* or residence, which most of the schools possessed. Many of them went away to school when they were seven, attending the primary school and living in the *asuntola* for eight or nine years.

To some large Lappish families it was a relief to have the children away and not needing support; but many felt the parting keenly. To them the family was the natural unit and they were very loyal to it.

After four years in the primary school some children left for a secondary school; the majority continued four more years in the higher part of the same school, then came to the continuation school in Ivalo to finish off their education. It was thus in contact with the whole commune, since every child not going to the secondary school passed through it.

There was a friendly atmosphere about the continuation school. It taught practical subjects, but the teachers had some freedom of choice and had introduced a short course in English. Pentti Mäenpää was one; Ulla Hauhia, who had been a hard-working secretary to the English Club, was another; and in charge was Ella Auer. Some Finns may be static and immobile when they speak; Ella Auer was not. She expressed what she said with all of herself; and she talked fluently. Her rooms had a touch of elaboration in their furnishing which in winter gave a needed contrast with the blank white outside. She was very generous, and we often received a little gift of something good to eat from her.

There were at that time twenty-three boys and thirteen girls in the continuation school; at my instigation Ulla asked some questions to find out what their attitude to life was and how school had affected them. Of the boys, six had Lappish as the home language, and two Kolta Lappish; some had their homes close to the road, but the farthest lived sixty miles from the road and the next farthest forty miles. They came from families having between one and ten children; most had over four.

When asked if they would prefer to live in Ivalo rather than the place where their home was, seventeen of the boys said clearly, "No," and five did not answer. When asked why, several answers showed that they preferred the kind of country where their homes were: "At home there are good views of the hills" . . . "There are no proper slopes here" . . . "There I can live alone and fish"—but one Lapp boy answered realistically: "The shops are too near here so that I spend all my money."

Eight of the boys thought they would like to stay at school longer; but none of these were Lapps. All the Lapps had had enough. The ambitions of the boys divided sharply along two main lines: some wanted to be reindeer men, others were clearly fascinated by mechanics; they either wanted work connected with cars, or to go to the workshop at Kaitakoski— across the border where the Finns were building a power station for the Russians.

Their comments on the *asuntola* life were, on the whole, favourable. Their chief reaction against it was on the ground of strictness: very free in their home surroundings, they resented rules, having to go to bed early, being limited as to where they could go. When asked what had been their greatest difficulty on starting school, the boys gave various answers, some of which might be given anywhere: "whether he could learn" . . . "getting used to discipline" . . . but some were peculiar to Lapland: "the long journey" . . . "too young to be in the boarding school" . . . and from a Lapp—"language".

But for the girls, almost without exception, the problem had been that of homesickness: of being away from home in the *asuntola*.

The present system of fixed schools has only been finally established in the last few years. In earlier days education was carried out by the Church, which sent round deaconesses who taught in the Lapp homes. Two of these, who had only stopped teaching a year or two ago, lived in Inari.

Ulla herself had more than one side to her nature. She was very interested in her work and the children and was learning Lappish—which few Finnish teachers attempt. But a gun hung in her room; occasionally she would go shooting. She was having a hut built for herself out in the wilds farther up the Ivalo River.

Toloskoski was the name of the stretch of river where Ulla's hut was situated. The river swirled round near there in a rocky S-bend, impassable by boat; to take a boat further up the river one had to drag it along the bank past the rocky stretch. On the more gently sloping bank of the river, with the forest behind and a superb view across the water to the other side where the bank rose up sharply, stood a hut belonging to a likeable, cheerful, informal character called Pentti Lahtinen.

Pentti Lahtinen, with his wife Else, ran the school at Törmänen, a few miles south of Ivalo, the place where the English Club held its first party. He was more than this, however. He was a force in the district—a member of the council, and secretary to the committee that looked after school affairs.

Pentti once came to us holding a copy of the magazine *Neuvostoliitto*. This is a magazine describing life and activities in the Soviet Union, and published by the Soviet Union in Finnish. "They send this round free to the schools," said Pentti. "Isn't there anything like it that we can get in Finnish about England?"

There wasn't; and there still isn't. It seems wrong that we are prepared to let the Finns have a clear picture of the achievements of the Soviet Union and a blank about England.

We had to complete two projects in connection with the schools before we left Ivalo: a final visit to Menesjärvi and a visit to Kaamanen, a village between Inari and Utsjoki. We were getting distinctly anxious about these; it was already October and we could not expect the snow to hold off much longer. Kaamanen was on the main road; but Menesjärvi, after the snow had fallen, was cut off—at least as far as a light car was concerned.

We took the road to the left at Inari one cold but still snowless afternoon. It was not, to us, a new road; but the stones seemed bigger and more ferocious in our own car—and it was very stony for most of the way. As we crawled along at twenty miles an hour or so we could hear them flying out on each side, with ever and anon an alarming thud as one slammed against the bottom of the car.

It was, however, quite a passable road, cut at intervals by small streams. Across these little ravines were wooden bridges.

At least . . .

Normally there were wooden bridges. At this particular time most of them were under repair, so that at intervals we found a great gap in the road with nothing linking it to the opposite side. As we approached, the two or three men working there would stop and hastily fling a couple of boards across, one for each side but only a few inches wide. I drove straight at them, hoping that my idea of where the wheels went was accurate, and by some kindly providence we landed on the other side and not in the stream below. At last, later than we had expected and after dark, we rolled down the steep rock-strewn hill near the lake and saw the welcoming lights of the school ahead.

Maija-Liisa and Matti welcomed us; and once inside the school there was a very cosy atmosphere. Living there had most of the comforts one could reasonably want; but in addition there was a special feeling of intimacy, of being with a tiny group of people separated from the world—or about to be. In the evening we sat round in the flat and talked with Maija-Liisa and Matti. Matti was planning to go elk-hunting; he would be away for several days, sleeping out with a tent. I asked if he found this uncomfortable in the low temperature; he said that once in winter he had had to sleep out on a bare mountain without a tent or fire, and after this he had had a cold. Otherwise it had not worried him. Matti was not a very bulky or heavy man; he had a much more intellectual type of build; but he was undoubtedly tough.

We talked a little about the prices of reindeer; Matti said that in the Menesjärvi district that year they had been selling for from 5,000 to 20,000 or 30,000 marks (£5 to a little over £30) depending on whether the reindeer were trained or not.

During this stay at Menesjärvi we also ran into a technical problem. We found that we had forgotten the spray, used to wash out the patients' mouths. This was a serious drawback to Arja. But Lapland encourages inventiveness. Fortunately we had one part of the spray, the part that went into the mouth, but not the other end that supplied the water; we had a car, however, and a car which was fitted with a windscreen washer, as required by Finnish law. After some engineering work and appropriate sterilization Arja was presented with a peculiar-looking but quite workable spraying equipment.

We could not finish all the work in one visit; we had to return to Ivalo for a short time and then come back to Menesjärvi. This time we were to find that we really had left it too late. We reached Menesjärvi safely on this return visit; but then difficulties began. Soon after we arrived the generator, which supplied the school with electricity, broke down. The caretaker disappeared into the cellar to work on it; and Arja's work became very difficult, since no electric light was available and we were now relying on an electric drill, a big improvement on the old foot-powered type, but helpless without power.

There was only one telephone in Menesjärvi, but by some system of communication of their own the Lapps had heard that the dentist was in action locally, and they began to arrive, lighting up the corridor outside the "surgery" with the blue and red of their clothing. Some had come before the breakdown; some were sent away; one Lappish girl who came with her husband had to be dealt with and her tooth was treated in the yellowish glow of a paraffin lamp. There was something very striking in the attractive young Lappish faces, the circle of warm light just adequate to show the mouth enough for Arja to work, and the deep blue and warm red of the Lappish clothing.

For most of my life I had accepted the weather, good or bad, without questioning how it arose; now, I became a keen student of the skies, looking for any sign of snow. I suddenly appreciated very keenly the way those who live in the wilder parts of Lapland move—not fixing a time to set out on a journey, but waiting for the moment when nature is co-operative; and once having started, not stopping till the object is reached. For this reason, a Lapp may lounge around doing nothing for days. He is not just being lazy; when the moment comes he will be off and then he may be out days and nights with very little rest.

Little clouds appeared on the edges of the sky; increased in number and moved towards the centre; finally closed up into a grey screen.

"How easily can the road get blocked?" I asked.

"The snow often comes and goes away at this time," said Maija-Liisa. "But the road can get blocked in a night, and it can stay all winter."

Then, one morning we woke up to find snow on the ground. Not much, only a thin layer; and throughout the day it melted away until after forty-eight hours it was gone. The sun shone in a cloudless sky once more.

That was the moment when we ought to have set off; but it seemed a pity to leave the dental work, now so near its end, incompleted, especially as the generator had now come to life again. The little clouds appeared again on the edges of the sky; swept inwards till they covered it; and the snow began again late in the afternoon. It went on all through the night, heavily, and when we woke in the morning there was a thick covering. It was not going away either; the sky was still full of it.

The work was finished; there was no prospect of the snow position improving; so that day we set out back home. The first hurdle was the hill, the steep hill down which we had come and up which we must go to get away from the school at all. It looked absolutely shocking: very steep; covered with snow; and slippery underneath with plenty of loose stones and irregularities to start a skid. The approach to it, also snow-covered and stony, restricted the possibility of approaching it at speed. Going as fast as we could I launched the car at the hill. We got about two thirds of the way up; at that point the wheels slipped sideways and the back slid off the road.

Then the whole school came streaming out, with ropes, led by Matti. They strung the ropes to the car, then with half in front pulling and the rest behind pushing, we climbed slowly over the brow of the hill. They gave us a final shove, and we were moving ahead on our own. Rather too much on our own; if anything went wrong there was no telephone along the road for fifteen miles and then it was some miles aside.

We ploughed along through the snow; but nothing else at all had been along the road and it was too thick for a light car. We had two or three miles on the level or downhill, which we negotiated successfully, but at the first uphill we slid off the road into the forest. Fortunately we did not hit any trees. We climbed out of the car and looked at it ruefully; it was impossible to get it back on the road without help, and even then it seemed unlikely that we could get through.

Matti came to the rescue—Matti and his Russian Pobeda. He had been so doubtful as to what would happen to us that he had followed in the car, together with another man. The Pobeda was a biggish, heavy car; its petrol consumption was high and it was not regarded in Finland as particularly chic to own one; but it was clearly built for rough, tough work. I was extremely glad to see it. I had had visions of showing how a light British car and a British driver could get even through these arduous conditions: but they did not become reality. After being hauled back on to the road we drove humbly in the wheel tracks of the Pobeda all the way to Inari. But we got home, with the car, and without having to wait for the spring.

Our final expedition was to Kaamanen. Kaamanen was a village between twenty and twenty-five miles north of Inari, close to where the Utsjoki road divided off from the road to Karigasniemi. In the beginning I was somewhat indifferent as to Kaamanen; but I found it had more queer and entertaining features than I had expected.

In Kaamanen, as in most of the schools in Inari commune, there were two teachers; but by some whimsy of fate, the male teacher at Kaamanen was called Adam, and the female teacher Eve. They had surnames as well, of course; but their first names seemed so suited that I could never think of them by any other. Both were quite young; they had not long finished their training; but occasionally Eve's eyes had a very old, knowing expression, as though she really had been acquainted with human life for a very long time.

Kaamanen had a similar plan to many of the schools: it consisted of the school building, above which were the teachers' flats, the residence for the children, and the service block containing the toilets and the electric generator. The generator kept respectable hours, starting up at half past six in the morning and shutting down at half past ten at night; usually the lights faded out on us before we were in bed and woke us up when they came on in the morning.

The teachers each had a three-room flat; the dental surgery was established in the kitchen of Adam's flat and we used another of his rooms as our bedroom. In travelling to the various schools the dentist was very much dependent on the hospitality of the teachers for her comfort, since it was usually in their rooms she had to live. The room which Adam had given us was warmed by a stove which went right from floor to ceiling; once or twice a day he would light a fire here and for several hours the heat stored would radiate itself comfortably into the room.

Most of the working hours were spent in artificial light. Soon after the electricity came on Adam would be up, and between seven and eight o'clock when we staggered out into the corridor he would offer us coffee. The room across the corridor altered its character rapidly in the early morning, changing from a kitchen for coffee making into a bathroom used for shaving and from that into a dental surgery. It would still be only faintly light when Adam and Eve went off to school and the first children appeared for treatment.

At eleven o'clock we all joined the children in the dining hall for the first main meal of the day, life-saving though not Ritzy; an hour or two later we met Eve and Adam for coffee; and then at four o'clock came the last main meal, again with the children. This was mid-November; it was pretty dark at three in the afternoon and really dark by four.

Adam and Eve had doubts as to how much they liked Kaamanen. Both she and Adam, however, were very keen to learn more English. They had studied it for three years at school, and spoke it rather hesitantly. They brought out all their books and we had an English lesson each evening.

"Could you give to the school an English lesson?" asked Adam.

"I don't mind. But how do you think they would take it?" I replied.

"They would like it," said Adam. He seemed very certain,

so I agreed. I had given many lessons to adults in Ivalo, and taught once or twice in the school, but this was the first time I had taken children as young as this who knew not a word of English.

They were from nine to thirteen years old, and thirty-eight were waiting in the classroom, half of them Lappish. I wondered what on earth their reactions to me were going to be. But they seemed to welcome the experiment; they repeated a few of the common words and phrases very co-operatively. There were one or two shy little girls at the younger end who scarcely dared to whisper and an odd boy or two flung his weight about, but on the whole the class kept together very well.

We had a second lesson the next day. I tried to teach them a few of the vital words such as "food", and if any English-speaking person is saved from dying of hunger anywhere near Kaamanen, I hope he will be grateful to me.

After the second meal at four o'clock in Kaamanen there was a long, timeless, changeless gap; one could hardly tell whether it was night or morning. Adam did once go to sleep at half past five in the evening; he woke up three hours later, looked at his watch, and in a panic started to hurry to school, thinking it was morning. The dawn, when it did come, was often beautiful—a red angel with a flaming sword slightly to the east of north.

Once or twice in the evenings we had a visitor, a quite uninvited visitor. We were sitting with Adam and Eve on our first evening there when the door of Adam's sitting room was thrown open. A young man stood just inside the door. He had the longest electric torch I have ever seen. He looked carefully round the room, studied us all closely, then saluted smartly and disappeared.

"Who's that?" I asked.

"The policeman," said Adam.

"But there's no policeman in Kaamanen. All the police are in Ivalo, apart from those in Utsjoki."

"He thinks he's a policeman," explained Adam. "He belongs to a family in the village. He's not quite right in the head. He's a nuisance sometimes, walking in like that."

"He is," said Eve. "He comes to my rooms as well."

"But couldn't you lock the doors of your flats?" I asked.

"Lock the doors!" they chorused in horror. "We couldn't possibly do that. What would people think?"

Sometimes just after mid-day I would go for a walk in the forest. From here a path led to Sevetti; in winter there was regular transport by the snow bus, a vehicle with tracks and skis at the front which could move over the snow. The lakes and rivers were partly, though as yet not completely, frozen. I wondered what I should do if I met a bear: one had been seen a mile or two away. I did not really expect such an encounter; it was likely to keep away from the village. Then I realized that my mind had worked out an answer: you couldn't tackle it, you couldn't run or climb faster than it could, but you could get out on the ice, which would be too frail to bear its weight but might stand yours. It was interesting to find how the mind could half unconsciously prepare some solution to a totally strange situation.

There are not many bears in Lapland nowadays: those wishing to shoot one sometimes offer considerable sums for particulars of a bear's den. Some regard the shooting of a bear by several men who simply wait for it to come out of its den as unsporting; Pandy described it as "murder".

The snow at Kaamanen had come, then partly gone, then come again. The roads were covered with ice with water on top. They were sanded, but there was a very long stretch of road to cover, so that frequently hardly any sand could be seen. On Saturday evening the work was finished, and we decided to set off home, although it was after eight in the evening. Saturday evening is a bad time to travel, since it is likely that any treatment of the roads will only be carried out at the week end if it appears very urgent. We thought, however, that it would be pleasant to wake up on Sunday morning in our own beds.

As soon as it reached the main road the car gave a snake-like skid. Arja looked at me; I altered my idea of the time it would take to reach Ivalo and kept on. The grip of the road on the wheels was minute. We crawled along carefully and with agonizing slowness; in places there was a drop at the side of the road which did nothing to make us feel happier; and after a couple of hours we saw the bridge at Inari. On no inch of the road would one have dared to touch the brake.

"Shall we stop here overnight?" asked Arja, as we approached Inari. She had (wisely) said hardly anything since we left Kaamanen.

"No," I told her. "I want to get back to our own home tonight."

Arja did not say very much more till we were some way past Inari and near to where the road ran along the lakeside. Then she suddenly said:

"What do I do if we go into the lake? Try to get out?"

It was a question with some point in it; we were at the worst time of the year, with frozen roads, but the lake ice was certainly not capable of supporting a car. Before I could think out an answer, we skidded again. I got out to test the road, and nearly fell down. I drove on even more soberly than before.

Then we met our Waterloo. The lakeside road was both twisty and hilly, and with memories of our Menesjärvi experience I was taking the hills very carefully. As I found out later, this is the wrong technique: you have to drive fairly fast up the hills, hoping you don't go off the road. We failed to surmount one hill, and instead skidded back. Perhaps the most unpleasant experience in a car is to be skidding backwards, unable to stop. We halted the car a foot or two from the edge —it just held on the footbrake—put a stone behind it, and Arja went to look for help. Fortunately we were not far from the power station. I stayed with the car.

Then I had a queer experience. I thought I saw a hooded figure on the opposite side of the road. The whole atmosphere was ghostly: midnight, loneliness, the dangerous road, a dog howling in the distance. For a moment I could have believed that this was a haunted spot at which motorists had perished regularly. I walked across to it, thinking: either this is going to turn itself into something else when I get near, or I'm going to enter a quite new region of experience. The ghost remained till I got half-way across the road, then suddenly became a white stone.

After that a man came from the power station with some sand, and the whole situation suddenly became very normal and reassuring. A friendly taxi happened along; the driver offered to take our car over the hill, and succeeded; he drove behind us till we reached Ivalo, and knowing that assistance was available I took all the hills fast and successfully. So, despite everything, we reached home.

The Ivalo taxi drivers were superbly skilful; several had been driving for many years without having an accident.

It was not always as bad as that, of course; most times we drove—as they say in Finland—quietly, and got through; but "the Kaamanen road" has become a symbol to Arja and myself of dangerous driving conditions, and to compare anything to "the Kaamanen road" suggests that it should only be traversed with extreme care, and preferably not at all.

ONCE more the road between Ivalo and Rovaniemi, the road which I had first travelled along almost exactly three years ago: but this time the highway was from, not to, the wilderness.

We were driving south on a December afternoon; and this time we should not turn at Rovaniemi, but go on towards Helsinki and, symbolically, Copenhagen and London. As far as we knew we should not return; we might come for a holiday, but we should no longer be an organic part of Lapland, the Inari commune dentist and the Englishman. If we did come— and they say that those who have been attracted to Lapland never escape—it would be as two different people.

I should not again see Lapland with quite the same eyes, puzzled and seeking, sometimes hopelessly lost, dimly conscious that somewhere here might be a signpost to what I was looking for. We could not again live those difficult, sweet years, the first years of Lilian's life. No moment in the future would be quite like the one in which I had stared down for the first time at that small golden-haired figure. I should not again cycle back through a summer evening with the sun still impossibly high in the sky and a little girl on the front of the bicycle, calling out "Home! *Kotiin!*" in her two fragmentary languages. I should not see her at the door of the *kämppä*, calling out "Walter! Walter!" with lovable impudence; or watch her, deceived by the skirt-like nature of the male Lappish costume, disturb an unusually large Lappish man by shouting "Lappish girl" in an embarrassingly clear voice.

There would be many gay and glorious moments in the future, there might be again the moments of childhood; but they would not be these particular moments—of the first three years of life in a Lapland setting. Of one thing I was certain: whatever doubts I might have about myself or my own actions, those years had been good for Lilian. Far from suffering from this distant northern environment, she had benefited. She was very healthy; she had hardly ever had a cold.

It had not been easy to get ourselves into the car on to that road. Splitting up a life into pieces and packing it away is in any case harrowing; and in Lapland one could not depute the whole job to a removal firm. However, our friends had been very kind. I had been down in the cellar for some time making up big wooden boxes, the wood for which had been presented to us by Gunnar from his saw mill. Later the carpenter from next door took this over and refused any payment for his work. At last the boxes had been filled, nailed together and sent off on the long aluminium-covered long-distance lorry that came twice a week to Ivalo; the house was an empty shell.

We had said good-bye to many people in the same way that we had met them, over coffee. It was the custom amongst the group of professional people to give a farewell party for those from among them who were leaving; we had been to several of these at other times; it seemed strange and sad to feel that we ourselves were now going. It was, nevertheless, a good party, with some picturesque moments.

With a certain fitness our life in Ivalo ended where it had begun: we spent the last night or two as guests of Eetu and Maija Saarelainen. There is a kind of dreaminess about Lapland; they say that a man will sometimes sit for days picturing what he is going to do but never starting it. The middle of winter, in which daylight is gone in a flash, is very conducive to this mood. It seemed to have touched us; the days went by with every day still a little left over for the next; it seemed impossible to leave Ivalo.

But, finally, we went. We drove a couple of miles out of Ivalo to the rubbish dump and tipped out all the old jars and bottles; then we went round to our friends distributing the plants which had graced our house; and about one o'clock in the afternoon we were ready to go. Our feelings were mixed: against the background of our regret at leaving Lapland we could hear the siren song of the soft seductive south, where the winter is short, where the apple trees blossom late in the year and the sun can be seen throughout the winter.

But in our case the "soft south" meant a hundred miles north of Helsinki.

We drove towards the crossroads with the Maja on the right, then left past Osuuskauppa, Henni's pharmacy, the post office, and our former flat; the road leading to Kalle's house; the turning to the headquarters of the frontier guards; then Ivalo was behind.

Lighting-up time at that season was two o'clock on a light day or half past one on a dark one. By the time we climbed up to Kaunispää the light was completely gone. Once more I was on that 180-mile stretch between Ivalo and Rovaniemi.

Once more, also, the darkness: again the world had shrunk to the silvery-yellow patch of light cast by the headlamps on the road. All around stretched out Lapland; I could picture it now though I could not see it—snow-covered hill rising through snow-covered forest, and snow-covered forest broken up by snow-covered lake until the horizon was reached. Somewhere out there the reindeer, threatened occasionally by bears and wolves, were being gathered together and were moving towards the round-up centres. And out there were people, like tiny stitches in a vast carpet, in little isolated homes in the wilderness.

What was it in Lapland that had appealed to me, and what now caught at my heart strings as we were leaving? I could almost hear a voice in my mind asking the questions.

"Wasn't it rather crazy to come to Lapland?"

Of course at times, many times, it looked so. It was no way to develop a steady career. I was no very great fishing or shooting man; I had no remarkable powers of endurance on skis or journeying through the forest. My talents had been developed along lines which required a complicated civilization for them even to be visible. But because of this very fact that I was in some ways so unsuited to the environment and yet felt its attraction—I conclude that there was in me some inner sympathy with Lapland. It had something I needed.

"And what was this quality—or these qualities—in Lapland which you needed and with which you were in sympathy?"

I thought of the way the eye glides over the landscape in Lapland, from one rounded hilltop to another, with nothing to stop it till it reaches the junction of earth and sky; and compared it with the rough way the city has, jerking the eye from one hard flat wall to the other, setting down so firmly the limits within which it is permitted to wander. I remembered the noise and competition of the city; I thought of quiet Lapland and the sound of the winds running through the branches, or the smooth moaning of the snow under the skis. I thought of the way men were straightforward in Lapland, saying what they thought and respecting independence.

"Good, of course; but if you only think of these things might it not all be escapism? Fleeing from the reality of the modern world? Was there anything that went deeper?"

Yes, there was, but it is difficult to describe; for most of my life I had been ignoring it. My life had been built up for many years with the object of developing reason and the intellect; for years I had tried to arrange life so that nothing happened which I could not understand and control—had thought, indeed, that to be the ideal. But in Lapland I had had the deep symbolical experience of losing the sun, of passing into the blackness—and of coming out again; of being lost in the forest,

cut off from all that had supported me previously and alone—
with what?For that there are no adequate words; I have largely
learned the language of reason, and here one must talk the
language of emotion and intuition. I was conscious of the sweep
of a great and powerful force: a force appealing to something
older and deeper than reason in man; and knew that I must
accept it or be crushed by it.

For me, perhaps, it would be a life-long battle between these
two—between reason and the forces which worked through
the emotions and the intuition; or better, a struggle to arrange
a way of living between them. But was this not also a basic
problem of our civilization—that the rational mechanical way
of thinking, used largely for sheer material gain, had become
the dominant and respected one; and our deeper needs,
squashed down and cut off from our acknowledged selves,
could only grow in intensity till they were liable to burst out
explosively and destroy us?

In the days before I went to Lapland I had partly looked on
our life as inevitable: an expression of the nature of man.
Now, having seen the Lapps, I was not so sure. They possessed
qualities we lacked. They were peaceful, not only in the sense
of not attacking others, but also in possessing an inner
quietude. They could wait; they had none of the nervous rest-
lessness which characterizes our city life. They thought their
own thoughts, sometimes profound thoughts, unbound by a
particular system; and they were not afraid to express these
thoughts. They were not constantly seeking to increase at the
expense of others.

But would the Lapps be allowed to keep their way of life—
and would Lapland be allowed to retain its deep, peaceful
character? Even during the three years we had lived in Ivalo,
there had been many changes. The road had been driven
through to Utsjoki; a water bus had begun to run up the lake
to Inari in summer; the planes had started to fly all the winter
to Ivalo; the hotel there had built a new block which doubled
its size; and the construction of a very-high-frequency radio
station had been started on the top of Kaunispää.

Lapland was changing rapidly; but did those who were
changing it know the value of what they were altering? The
process of change went with the road; it was like an organism
creeping over the landscape, ever and anon pushing out a finger
into the forest, re-shaping everything it met there. But whilst
it might bring "comfort and convenience" this process could
also destroy; it could take away the freedom and independence
of the Lapps and make them slaves of the factory hooter. Un-

necessarily: for reindeer keeping is for many of them a sound and economic livelihood.

And, if the way of life of the Lapps were destroyed, it would destroy what we need to study and incorporate into ourselves and our effective but unbalanced civilization.

These thoughts were in the air as we continued along the road in the winter darkness; not all clearly realized at the time, for the Lapland experience was like a seed which grew. Soon the windows of the car had all frosted over so that only two port holes on the windscreen remained; and the dip switch had frozen up. But there was little traffic about; we did not meet more than one or two other vehicles in each hour; and near Rovaniemi we overtook the Bear, its light standing out in the darkness amidst a flurry of snow.

We stayed in Rovaniemi overnight.

It was well on in the morning and quite light when we left Rovaniemi. It was a good road to Kemi and we drove steadily on. I should have expected what was going to happen, I should have remembered what we had lost; but I didn't, and it came as a surprise, almost a shock. Suddenly we reached the top of a hill—and there, ahead, was the sun: not an ordinary sun, not a clear small disc, but a huge, hazy, majestic semicircle on the horizon. It had been there all the time; the whole world had not been in darkness, but only a part of it, and we had driven back into the light again. Though we had not been able to see it, the sun had been there, would always be there, and we could find it again when we wanted to.

We had still a long way to go and it was not all sunshine on the way. Much of the driving was in darkness, over roads which were unknown to us, often with nothing visible except the white arrows of the snow storm shooting towards us in the light of the headlamps. But the shock of that sudden vision remained. Darkness and light! They could symbolize many things: evil and good; the known and the unknown. For me, perhaps, light was the clear cold perception of the brain, and darkness the medium which held the mysterious creative forces of the emotions and the spirit. At that moment of revelation I felt a sudden freedom, an ability to move from one to the other. I was a creature of both.

Glossary of Finnish and Lappish Names

PLACE NAMES in Finnish Lapland are confusing at first sight since in addition to its Finnish name a place may also have a Swedish name, or a Lappish one: and sometimes all three. Thus Inari on some maps is Enare; Haaparanta is also Haparanda; Karesuando on the Swedish side becomes Kaaresuvanto on the Finnish side, where it is also spelt Kaarresuvanto.

Many Finnish place names have an ending which indicates some physical feature; for example *joki*, as in Utsjoki, means "river". A glossary of these and other words mentioned in the text or which may be encountered is given below.

järvi	a lake.
joki	river.
johtaja	the leader or head of an enterprise. Used very widely.
kelkka	a seat on runners.
kunnanjohtaja	the chief appointed administrative official of a country district, or *kunta*.
kunta	*Kunta* may be translated as "commune"; it has no connection with Communism.
kämppä	a hut, usually in some remote spot.
koski	a rapidly-flowing stretch of water.
lahti	a bay.
maja	a place providing accommodation for travellers, ranging from a hotel to a hostel.
matkustajakoti	a place providing accommodation of good standard but with less elaborate service than a hotel, and usually not major meals.
polkku	a path.
ruska	the very special colouring of the Lapland landscape during the short autumn.
saari	an island.
tunturi	Higher than a hill and lower than a mountain; sometimes translated "fell".

Index

Note : The Finnish letters ä and ö come at the end of the alphabet